Martin Luther

The Great Reformer

Edwin P. Booth

Edited and abridged by
Dan Harmon

A BARBOUR BOOK

ISBN   1-55748-727-8

Published by   Barbour and Company, Inc.
                    P.O. Box 719
                    Uhrichsville, OH 44683

Printed in the United States of America.

Martin Luther

one

Planting

IRON MINES
1483-1497

O N THE MORNING of November 11, 1483, Bartholomew Rennebrecher, the parish priest of the Church of St. Peter in Eisleben, baptized the day-old son of Hans and Margaret Luther.

It was St. Martin's Day. True and devout Catholics that they were, the father and mother offered the name *Martin* for their firstborn. Father Rennebrecher took the baby in his arms, touched his fingertips in the holy water in the fine old font, and laid them gently on the boy's head. ". . . .in the name of the Father and of the Son and of the Holy Ghost, Amen." The sign of the cross, ancient symbol of glory and humility, he marked on the little forehead to ward off the devil and all his works.

Margaret was glad to have the baby under the protection of Mother Church. She took seriously the great struggle between the unseen worlds and sought, as best she knew how, to hold true to her Catholic faith.

The service over, Hans carried the baby home again. As she looked at her boy, Margaret Luther knew her life had now begun in earnest.

Hans Luther, strong and determined but not ungentle, had come up from the land, son and grandson of peasants. He had courted Margaret in the town of her birth and girlhood, Eisenach. She thought of its lovely hills and valleys. One hill in particular, crowned with its glorious Wartburg, possessed her thoughts, as it did every son and daughter of Eisenach.

Her people had been burghers; his had been peasants. The Zieglers were not sure the marriage was a good one for her, preferring a union with an established Eisenach family. But she was not afraid of life with him, for they had talked long and often about the way in which, forsaking the land of the mines, they would work their way steadily up in life. They would stay a while now in Eisleben, until the little fellow was more ready for traveling, and then they would move on to the center of the mining area and set up their home.

Hans Luther worked daily in the mines of Eisleben. He had been reared on the land in Mohra with older and younger members in the family. By the custom of his people, the home and land in Mohra would fall to the youngest son, not the eldest. So Hans had known for a long time that he must cut his own path. In journeys to Eisenach he had met and loved Margaret Ziegler and now knew the fruition of their love in marriage, a home and a son. He wasn't quite sure how it would go in the mines, but he seemed to sense the fitness for the work and did not hesitate.

Hans was sturdy and fearless. He honored the church, was devout in his religious practices, and believed, as had his people for many generations, in the grand dogmas of an otherworldly Christianity. He must keep his courage stout and fight for sustenance for himself and his family. The devil would do strange and unexpected things; the mines were treacherous; plagues would come—but he would make for himself a place of respectability in the world he knew. So in firm spirit, with confidence in his ability to work his way through, Hans was laying the foundation of his family security. When he carried the boy to the priest for the baptism, he felt strong and content.

Hans and Margaret were living in a common house, small and dark, on a narrow, unpretentious street. It was near the great St. Peter's Church. Eisleben had about 4,000 inhabitants in the year the Luthers lived there, having grown rapidly from a village of 500 after the opening of the mines. They were comparative strangers, having no relatives there and few friends. Their residence in Eisleben would give it a rich and lasting renown, but all they thought of toward morning of the eleventh of November was their firstborn.

Through the winter months of 1483-84 Hans worked, Margaret kept house, and the baby grew. Eisleben did not satisfy the hopes of the family, and in the early summer they moved to Mansfield. Here they were in the center of one of the mining districts, and here Hans could hope to lease a mine of his own.

This was a happier, livelier town. The counts of Mansfield, living in a fine stone castle on a neighboring hill, guarded the town's prosperity and encouraged its workmen. Hans may well have known the saying that was current in the town, "Whom the Lord loves, He causes to live in Mansfield." But the early months and years in Mansfield were not easy for Hans and Margaret.

As Martin grew into the years when memory begins its work, he saw his mother bringing firewood from the forest beyond the village, saw the heavy load bend her back to its weight, saw the slow steps that brought her near the house, and heard the sigh of relief when the pile slipped from her shoulders to the ground by the door. It was the common lot of the workman's wife to carry wood from the forest. Meanwhile, Hans' hold on work and reward grew steadily stronger, and the future held some promise as they daily carried on their routines. Martin was fascinated by the brothers and sisters who came to share the family love.

The father and mother early instituted a rigorous but fair discipline. Obedience was exacted, and Martin knew, often to his discomfort, that neither parent would let offenses go unpunished. Conflict between the straight-seeing, decisive Hans and the boy was, of course, inevitable. Slight offenses by the boy were punished severely. Martin carried the resentment against his father for hours and days—only to be won back to love when a new day brought new interest and new companionship.

The home was oriented along thoroughly Christian lines. The vigor of the Thuringian* custom—not the absence of love or the exercise of brutality—was responsible for the parents' severity. Martin certainly feared his father and mother, but the fear was grounded in the knowledge of certain retribution following undesirable activity. The love that lighted the home in Eisleben in November 1483 never was absent from the home in Mansfield as the years went by. The newer children were as well-loved as Martin, and the whole atmosphere

*Luther was born at Eisleben in Thuringe, Saxony.

carried a sense of protection and affection into the lives of the children.

Long afterward, Luther was to say, in the manner of an oracle, that his boyhood fear drove him into the monastery. That is the theologian talking. This boyhood fear was the great and strangely lovely experience in human life where a father and mother throw their earnestness in the corrective rearing of their child. The love of Hans Luther would follow Martin through difficult experiences few fathers face, and it would never falter.

Hans and Margaret were building their lives well in Mansfield. Many a quiet evening must have seen the Luther family in happy companionship. The background of that great family life in Wittenberg years later must have been here in Mansfield. Long winter evenings around the great, decorated porcelain stove and long summer evenings sitting through the twilight marked the little hearts gathered around Hans and Margaret with family love.

Taught by his mother, Martin learned the Lord's Prayer, wondering often what it was all about. He waited for the years to give it meaning. The Ten Commandments he slowly mastered, reciting them to a father and mother who taught him that in the breaking of any of them he would earn a terrible, eternal punishment. The Apostles' Creed, too, they taught him—valiant words they understood little themselves, but words upon which their church was built, words as lovely coming from the stumbling memorization of the little boy as from the chant of the cathedral choir. They told him of the God Who creates and governs, Who watches, rewards, and punishes. They told him of the Christ who came for his salvation, and they sang with him the infinitely tender and pathetic Christmas songs of Thuringian tradition. His lips early formed the lovely *"Uns kommt ein Schiff geladen,"** as the lips of our own children form the equally lovely "Away in a Manger."

Through song and picture, he learned of the little Christ of love and the supreme Christ of judgment. His parents taught him that Christ sits to judge the living and the dead; He will exact from His people the holy life, and dreadful is His wrath. When they took Martin to church each week, he looked with strange and ever-growing intelligence upon a sword-holding, thunder-visaged Christ on a rainbow in the great stained-glass window. They told him of the saints who in tender mercy would help him if he would only call upon them, interceding for him with the great Judge.

Slowly, as he grew, these strong teachings became fixed in his mind. He was early apprised of the existence of the spirit world. His otherwise self-sufficient father was sure of the work of the devil and the need for saints. Martin saw his mother's face when she knelt before the crucifix, and he felt it must be some holy power indeed to bring such strange beauty to her whom he knew so well. He heard both father and mother appeal with fervor and sincerity to St. Anna, protectress of the miners, and in his own way he breathed many a prayer to her, too.

The years before he went to school were filled with normal play and work, with the teachings of the ancestral faith, with the fear of punishment and the fear of God, with the unquestioned absorption of traditional piety, and with wholesome love and honor for his parents.

While he grew, his father rose to a place of respect and

---

*German, roughly translated, "a ship is coming"

affection in the town. Hans was friendly with the priest at the church, sang lustily and well at the church festivals, and maintained an ever-increasing connection with all the affairs of the parish. When Martin was eight and in the first year of school, his father was elected to the town council and continued with distinction to serve in this capacity until his death.

The burden of poverty began to lighten, for Hans now was leasing mines and smelting furnaces to operate for himself. So they prospered, and Martin entered the common school in Mansfield as the son of an independent and respected family.

We shall never know what Margaret Ziegler Luther thought on that morning in 1490 when her little boy walked down the narrow, crooked street to the town square and turned to enter the school. Perhaps the other children at home took her attention so quickly from Martin that she didn't meditate long. But the boy was walking into a different world.

Latin—not the boys of Mansfield—was the object of the school's existence. The methods were strict and brutal, the teachers ignorant and unsympathetic, the entire atmosphere one to charge any boy's mind with thorough dislike and even hatred. To memorize slowly and without interest the rules of Latin grammar from that thousand-year-old textbook of Donatus, to be beaten by the assistant for faulty memory as well as for breaks in discipline, to be forced to talk in Latin instead of German—this became Martin's lot. There were great days of excitement and interest, of course, when the church festivals came around and the whole town turned out to celebrate. But the burden of the school was always on the boys.

Neither stupid nor rebellious, Martin moved in a fair way through his early schooling. He sang with the sons of rich and poor alike in many a street serenade and many a church choir. His clothes and his food were typical, and he was content. But the Mansfield school was not where his interest lay. His interest was where his brothers and sisters were growing up, where his father would sing to him and tell him stories. Lovely indeed is the picture, drawn long afterward by Martin, of his father laughing. Here is revealed the true Hans Luther with the burden of the day removed and the sternness of discipline relaxed, while friendship, family life, and deep good humor lightened up the evening.

While Martin sat through the school year during his late second and early third class, with his teachers doing their best to hold his mind to the dreadful routine of grammatical rules, events of almost unbelievable importance were happening elsewhere. In 1492, the world into which he had been born was passing away. While he mastered the old declensions, Columbus' sailors looked in mingled terror and hope at endless miles of water. While he ran from school to play, Lorenzo the Magnificent lay dying in Florence; when he died, so did the city-state which had been the glory of the Renaissance. While Martin gathered wood from the forest and set the yard in order, Rodrigo Borgia ascended St. Peter's throne to bring to a climax the deadly secularization of the church these northern peasants loved so well.

While Martin listened to the evening conversation of his home, another home in far-away Spain rejoiced in the coming of a little son named Ignatius. While Martin played at warfare with the boys of Mansfield, the combined armies of Ferdinand and Isabella, in a last charge of knighthood, drove the Moors from Spain and set the Christian flag above Granada. While he watched his mother care for his little brother, another mother was taking care of two little brothers named Arthur and Henry, and her husband, Henry VII, was nationalizing England. Toward the close of the year, Martin might have heard some neighbor tell his father that Maximilian was to be the new emperor of the Holy Roman Empire, to which his people owed allegiance.

The world was fixed and stable for him and his Mansfield elders, but while they taught its flatness and immobility to the little Luther, the eyes of Copernicus were poring over his books in his second year at the University of Cracow. Little ships and great men were moving, thrones were rising, ancient truths were falling—while in Mansfield, nine-year-old Martin learned his Latin, sang his folk songs, loved his family, and dreamed the dreams of boyhood.

ANCESTRAL MUSIC
1497-1501

Through the winter of 1496-97 Hans Luther talked often with a friend, Reinicke, about their sons. Hans' oldest boy, Martin, was now thirteen, and Reinicke's oldest son, John, was nearly the same. The boys had been together through the work of the Mansfield schools, and it was now time that they should either continue in school in some larger town or abandon their schooling and go to work. Hans wanted Martin to continue his studies, since he showed promise of being able to work in one of the professions, possibly law.

In the neighboring town of Magdeburg, much larger than Mansfield, were good schools. There, too, was a mutual friend, Paul Mosshauer, who could receive the boys. Their childhood was over. Educational custom called for a change of school every so often, and it was time for the boys to take the open road and test their courage and ability in competition. So the fathers agreed to send their sons off together to the school in Magdeburg.

Martin and John heard the decision gladly. They had been close friends and were to remain so through life. They looked forward eagerly to Magdeburg.

Some money was available, but not much, and it would be the boys' task to help as best they could with begging and street singing. These were normal activities of "wandering students." Special laws exempted students from the regular civil police power and gave them certain freedoms.

Their clothes were arranged in the lightest possible bundle, to be strapped on their backs. Shoes were set in order for the walk to Magdeburg. Food was prepared. Letters to Paul Mosshauer were written. Money was provided, and they were ready.

Martin bade good-bye to his father, mother, brothers and sisters, settled his pack, picked up his walking stick, joined John Reinicke, and headed away from Mansfield along the narrow winding road.

He was strong and well-grown when he started out that Easter season of 1497. Well-disciplined at home, he was usually in control of a quick and powerful temper. Naïve, spontaneous, he laughed heartily. He enjoyed life. Religious in the way of his people, he relied on the word of his parents and priests for the truth of the Christian faith in which he had been reared. Sensitive to beauty, he knew the native flowers of Mansfield, loved its fields and forests, and looked with quiet contentment on its hills.

What we call roughness and coarseness in speech and action were, in him and his companions, normal expressions. Compared with his people and his time, Martin was more sensitive to beauty and the things of the spirit than the average boy of thirteen. There was no brooding, abnormal moroseness, no sullen rebellion against the discipline of home and school. He was not independent of his father's will in major decisions of life, nor did he desire to be. The trip to Magdeburg was his father's will, so Martin moved in honorable fear of his father's judgment, and he lived with firm assurance of his family's support.

The walk was not long, and the boys were strong and enthusiastic. In Magdeburg they found shelter in Mosshauer's home. Where Martin lived during his year in Magdeburg we do not know exactly, but it's possible Mosshauer offered both boys shelter for the entire period. They sang on the streets for their bread. Martin's voice and his feeling for music were exceptionally good and would bring him enjoyment throughout his life. Yet it was not easy to secure a good living, and there is reason to believe that in Magdeburg he learned from experience, as he had never known at home, what poverty and hunger could mean.

Magdeburg had a fine, large cathedral, built toward the close of the twelfth and opening of the thirteenth centuries. The citizens were proud of its exceptional architecture. It was the seat of the archbishop and was prominent in the affairs of church and state.

Attached to the cathedral, in the custom of the period, was a well-known and popular cathedral school. The normal course of study of the advanced Latin school was pursued. Logic, rhetoric, dialectic, doctrine, and theology were additional studies Mansfield had not taught.

Martin became a regular scholar of the cathedral. In the cathedral choir he took his place and absorbed the mighty liturgy of his church. More important than all else in this new school was a new emphasis by his teachers. He never quite forgot the harshness of the municipal grammar school teachers in Mansfield, but here he was taught by the well-loved Brethren of the Common Life.

Founded in Holland, about 1380, on the gentle piety of Gerhard Groote and his first disciple, Florentius Radewijns, the Brotherhood had two objectives: education and social service. Groote had begun both in his own lifetime, and the advance had been rapid. Groote had met his death ministering to sufferers of the Black Plague.

In education, the Brotherhood almost invariably entered existing schools as teachers rather than setting up new schools of their own. They were more intent on the growth of their pupils in Christian character than learning. Under their immediate instruction, a new world of sympathy and companionship must have opened up for the Mansfield boy.

The Brethren touched and trained more of the leaders of the Reformation period than any other teaching group. Erasmus, Calvin, Loyola, John Sturm of Strassburg, and a host of others knew the steady pressure of the quiet, learned Brethren. Thomas à Kempis was a Brother and set down the order's regular ideals. Thomas wrote the first biography of Groote, in whose footsteps he strove to follow.

Day after day throughout the fall and winter of his fourteenth year, Martin pursued the paths of education under the watch of men devoted to the teaching profession, absorbing from them far more in spirit and intuition than he ever realized. Magdeburg was filled with other church orders, too, and the boy became familiar with the strange, lovely devotion of the ascetics, who scorned the world and sought severe discipline.

With his family ambition and his respect for the socially superior, Luther was disturbed one day to see in the streets of Magdeburg a prince from the house of Anhalt humiliating himself by begging. The prince was insufficiently clothed, tired, and emaciated, struggling to create the "good deeds" of penitence. How strange it seemed to Martin, when princes walked in the pathway of beggars!

The Brethren taught him the pure Catholic faith. They were not among the heretical, and they did not lay in Luther's mind the foundations for any subsequent rebellion against doctrine. But they set in his life, by example and precept, the precious essence of the church's historic piety. To live in sincere simplicity, avoid sin, take duty seriously, serve fearlessly the commands of conscience, refuse wealth and position, scorn sin in high places, and feel the mystic satisfaction available to the Christian in prayer—these marked their daily lives. They were simple and obedient in doctrine. In life, they were quiet, controlled and sincere.

This quiet goodness and firm peace sank deeply into Luther's nature. He was happy in school here and prospered in study and character. But the bread was hard to earn, there was no relative nearby, and he often longed for the coming of summer and his return to Mansfield.

When he went back home, he had grown, his Latin was better, and his habits were more regular. When Hans and Margaret talked of further schooling, his eyes lit up, and he spoke with great enthusiasm of the studies and of the men who had been his teachers in Magdeburg.

Margaret remembered her own people and her home in Eisenach and suggested he go there for a year. Her people could keep an eye on him, and he could roam the streets she loved so well. There were three fine churches there, many monasteries, and so much religious organizational activity that one in ten persons was in the business of the church. The Luthers were not dissatisfied with the year at Magdeburg, but Eisenach seemed a better place for their son.

John Trebonius was headmaster at the school attached to the Church of St. George. To Trebonius Martin Luther would owe a lifelong debt of gratitude. Trebonius taught in the late medieval style, with lecture and question, textbook and recitation. But he possessed the great teaching gift to inspire the student. So sensitive was Trebonius to the possibilities in his students that he and his assistants would lift their hats when they entered the older classes, recognizing the future greatness in their scholars.

Under Trebonius, Luther found new life and enthusiasm in the grand old studies of the medieval Latin school. The strange new world of the "humanities" was not opened to him; that was to come in Erfurt. But here the old world of grammar, rhetoric, and dialectic was taught with expert skill, and he was ever grateful.

Eisenach brought him many things outside of school. His relatives were not unkind, and one of them, Conrad Hutter, seems to have won young Martin to affection. Other families also entered his life. As in Magdeburg, he sang on the streets and accepted bread in return. But he did not have to depend on singing and begging for a living.

Where he lived the first year we do not know, but it was probably in the regular student lodging house. Soon after the first year he found a place with one of two families. The Schalbes, wealthy and prominent, took him under wing. They were greatly interested in religious activity and supported a foundation for one of the monastic orders called the Kollegium. Luther was well known to the monks of this Kollegium; he spent a great deal of time with them, and to them he was indebted for many permanent influences. The Schalbe family set the church and devotion far above all else in life.

Another family, the Cottas, also captured his heart. The story that Frau Cotta took him in when he was poverty-stricken and starving is untrustworthy. Better is the story that she heard him sing in the church choir and, taking a fancy to him, invited him—in proper Eisenach fashion—to her home. In this home he learned the grace of Thuringian custom; before, he had known its rougher aspects. Here hè sang the traditional folk songs of his people, folk songs of the free, natural life unrestricted by religious tradition. He laughed and drank and danced, and knew the open freedom of a beloved circle of friends.

Frau Cotta had a genius for friendship and for the gentility that makes an evening pass in harmony and happiness.

So the coarser habits of Mansfield and Magdeburg were softened considerably as the three years sped by at Eisenach. There were trips home to visit the family, then the return to school and friends, and Martin's life was happy.

St. Elizabeth was especially revered by the people of Eisenach. Born with rank and wealth, she had heard the higher call of Christian poverty as demonstrated by the blessed Francis of Assisi. Forsaking the possibilities of her social station, she had donned the robe of the Third Order of St. Francis and spent her life in service to the sick and needy. Hospitals, monastic houses, and churches bore witness to her lasting fame, but deeper than these memorials was the ever-present affection of Thuringian hearts for her sweet spirit.

In youthful, idealistic fashion, the now chivalric mind of Martin Luther was captivated by the otherworldly beauty of the saint. He thought often of the superior quality of the consecrated life and the inferior quality of the normal life.

But the warm-hearted Ursula Cotta wouldn't let him stray far from the ordinary. She reminded him often of the equally lovely value in the life of love and marriage.

Another friend touched his life deeply in Eisenach. John Braun, vicar of St. Mary's Church, was a man of rich and varied experience. Many years older than Luther, he befriended the students at Eisenach. They would gather at his rooms for long evenings of conversation and singing. He was a fine musician and taught Luther much.

Music had interested Martin since his early youth. He had been in church choirs at Mansfield, Magdeburg, and Eisenach. Now John Braun was giving him systematic and affectionate leadership. They played different instruments and sang far into the night.

Braun was a man of deep religious experience. Luther found himself taking for granted the supreme desirability of the religious calling. Braun must have told him many times of the struggles that preceded and the deep peace that followed his own decision to take Holy Orders. And Luther must have walked home at night through the quiet streets of Eisenach turning over in his mind the all-important question: Would he, too, be a priest? On occasion when he reached a temporary decision to serve the church and God, he must have walked with light step and singing heart.

But then the morning would come with the old interests all around him, and he would put off the day of decision into the future. His father had his heart set on the law, and that was enough for the present.

He would walk into the lovely valleys and drink again and again of their powerful earthly beauty. He knew here, as he had at Mansfield, all the flowers and animals that made these valleys their home. And lifting his eyes to the gray, great castle of Wartburg, he would dream of the strength of Teutonic arms against the enemy, dream of the ethereal beauty of St. Elizabeth, dream of the day when they held the contest of the minstrels here. But he did not yet dream that God was to be to him like "ein feste Burg,"* and that these castle walls would hide him from the wrath of a Spanish emperor and Italian pope.

----

*German meaning "a strong castle"

His mind and heart were growing steadily, yet the strange superstitions of the countryside were to him as real as to the humblest peasant. These Thuringian beliefs were set deep into his nature.

And the Eisenach of Luther's day held some strange ideas. A splinter of wood from a bed in which St. Elizabeth had slept was said to heal a toothache. Cripples were reputedly made whole by the power of the saint's relics. An indulgence could be had if one visited the grave of Heinrich Raspe, a man of unusual holiness. At the Dominican Cloister was an image of the Virgin Mary and Child, and when suppliants came, the Child was said to turn toward them or a way, depending on whether they brought a gift sufficiently large.

These countless religious superstitions were mixed with countless "old wives' tales." It was a strange, dark world, and the devil moved through it secretly. One was thought to be secure only by the constant use of the saints and the means of salvation provided in the church and its traditions.

Luther's mind was solid and terrifically honest. Once the beliefs of his boyhood were confirmed in serious study, as they were at Eisenach, the future could not wholly eradicate them. He was to remain a child of the light and darkness of his Eisenach world.

His days there were happy. When they came to an end, it was hard to part with the Schalbes, the Cottas, Conrad Hutter, John Braun, and other friends. But Erfurt, the greatest of late medieval German universities, lay just ahead, and Martin in his eighteenth year was ready to go.

two

Springtime

Monastery Gates
1501-1505

NEARING ERFURT, WALKING from Eisenach, Martin watched for the first sight of the city spires. He was eager to see the largest and most important city in Thuringe with its great cathedral towers. With more than one hundred major buildings devoted to professional religion, Erfurt had earned the title "Little Rome." Luther stepped jubilantly into this new world.

Erfurt in the early sixteenth century was Germany's greatest university. The old scholastic interests were well-represented on the faculty, but there also had grown up a fine center of the newer humanistic studies, and the combination had brought renown to the school. Attached to the major department of arts were the schools of law and theology.

Hans Luther was ready for his son to begin his final studies. Having prospered in the mines, Hans was now able to pay Martin's full expenses.

Martin lived at the student dormitory called the "Burse of St. George." Here was where most of the boys from Thuringe lived, and Luther would be among his own. He came in May 1501, procured his room, and went up to the university offices to register. His name appears on the university books as "Martinus Ludher ex Mansfield." He paid his tuition in cash and settled down to his new life.

Registering in the faculty of arts, he set himself up for the bachelor's degree. His studies now introduced him to philosophy. Under the guidance of professors Trutvetter and Usingen, he accepted the positions of the followers of William of Occam, a system saturated with Aristotelian thought. To the normal lectures in rhetoric and its kindred arts were added those in arithmetic, the natural sciences, ethics, and metaphysics. It seemed to Luther to be a self-contained and quite intellectually satisfying world.

But he met another world entirely in the poets and humanists who were bringing renown to Erfurt. He never was able to spend the time in these latter studies that he wanted to, for the routine kept him at work. He did, however, become familiar with the mood of the humanists and with the Renaissance-style poetry of the very popular Baptista Mantuan. Among his fellow students, during leisure hours, he heard the exaltation of humanism and enjoyed a philosophy more human and lovely than that of the scholastics. But his training in dialectics had been precise, and he never quite shook it off, remaining through life somewhat of a master in that art.

He was an excellent student. At his promotion to the bachelor's degree in 1502 he held a respectable ranking, and two years later, at his masters graduation, he was second in a class of seventeen.

Life at Erfurt University was what he had known and

anticipated. His Catholicity was unquestioned; his philosophy that of his teachers; his use of Latin and of the processes of dialectic unaltered.

But now, at eighteen, other and deeper currents were moving in his soul. He had been away from the direct influence of his home since he was fourteem. During these years he found himself struggling with the major problems of life. There had been security in following his father's strong will. That will had held the family safe during hard years of poverty. It had reared Martin through boyhood in a strict discipline. It had directed his work through the Mansfield grammar school and sent him on to Magdeburg. It had chosen Eisenach for his three-year schooling. It had furnished the incentive and money for the great privilege to attend Erfurt University. It had destined him for the law. But now young Luther was seeing things a little differently.

He had lived those earlier years without much thought of conflict. Now, as he matured, he was disturbed by the call of other interests unknown to his father. His native religious sensitivity began to assert itself. He thought again and again of John Braun's devotion to his sacred calling at Eisenach.

There was a great preacher in the Erfurt Cathedral who often left with Luther a divine restlessness. The mighty cathedral organ, the wonder of Thuringe, spoke to him with an unnamed, unknown power. Slowly, through these student days, came the vision of the eternal calling. He was happy, carefree, enjoying student fellowship and singing as always, but the problem was forming. He was thinking deeply of the horrors of sin and its punishment.

He had good cause to think of it. His father had never

minimized this part of life. His mother lived in terror of the unknown punishments of eternity. His people dwelt in continual fear of hell's torment. His church taught him constantly of the anger and wrath of God, of the judgment of Jesus.

And then there came to mind the great salvation in which he had been reared to believe. His father and mother had taught him of this, too. They had taught him of the grace of God and the mercy of Jesus, taught him of the favor of the saints. He could remember all the miners living on the hope of St. Anna, their protectress, and all the good people of Eisenach relying on the intercession of St. Elizabeth. His parents had taught him the value of good works, taught him reliance on the priesthood and deep faith in the church. His father walked uprightly and lived in honor, carrying the doctrines of Catholicism close to his heart.

So Luther fought the great battle. As the months of study drew to a close, he faced the possibility of entering professional school. It seemed to Hans that the climax of long planning was almost at hand, but to Martin the air was charged with uncertain terror. He clearly felt a religious calling, but he had always followed his father's will, and these two things were warring in his mind.

Happiness for a night would help him forget, but the morning found the problem unsolved. Steady work at his books and the routine of university life could not quiet the storm within him. To discuss it at home or write to his parents about these feelings seemed impossible. He did not know how to approach Hans on any issue of disagreement.

The day came for him to be awarded the master's

degree. He was elated by the procession in cap and gown through the streets of Erfurt to the convocation. But he could not forget as he walked that some of the boys who had come thus far through school with him were dead or dying from the plague that had ravaged the town in the spring of 1505. Like many another serious student, Luther found that life takes on a new meaning with the approach of death.

Also in his mind were the books of the philosophers on one hand, seemingly at odds with the simplicity of the Bible—which he had come to know at Erfurt—on the other.

Despite his apprehension and native dislike for law, Martin followed the wishes of Hans and entered the faculty in May 1505. He was under obligation, with his master's degree, to teach two years in the faculty of arts, but this did not preclude his own studies.

Hans was proud of his boy and addressed him formally. His commencement gift to his son was a copy of the expensive but necessary *Corpus Juris.*

In June Martin, now nearly twenty-two, left school to visit his home. We do not know why—possibly because the plague was so bad at Erfurt, or possibly because he wanted to talk with Hans about his distaste for the law— but on the return from this visit, he later wrote, as he came near the village of Stotterheim, he was caught in a thunderstorm and knocked from his horse by lightning. Fearing instant death, he vowed his life to the monastic calling if St. Anna would save him.

Yet the decision undoubtedly had already been made when the lightning bolt surprised him into acknowledging it. Through years of training he had been moving this

27

way. Many a hand had helped guide him. The lightning and the nearness of eternal judgment only broke the power of his father's will. Perhaps it substituted another, greater will than his father's—the will of the church.

Luther evidently was at peace as he continued the journey from Stotterheim to Erfurt, despite indications that he regretted the vow. One cannot move forward as rapidly as he did now, defying the pressure of home and friends, unless he has won peace within himself. Luther immediately ended his studies and sought admittance to the monastery.

He chose the Augustinian order. Founded in the mid-thirteenth century, it had been split by a quarrel between lax and strict observers of the order; the monastery in Erfurt was of the stricter branch. The vicar-general of the Saxon Province, in which Erfurt lay, was John von Staupitz, a man known for gentle piety and ordered life. The local congregation was widely known for strictness and honor in its vows and obligations. It had a highly reputed theological school. To Luther, studying theology in the peace of the monastic life was a vision of paradise.

On the evening of July 16, he called some of his friends to his rooms. They feasted, drank, and sang. Luther was the happy, warm spirit they had long known. Then he told them that the next day he was to enter the Augustinian monastery. In tears, they pleaded against his decision, but his heart was set.

On July 17, with his friends accompanying him, he walked down the familiar streets of Erfurt to the long, high wall that enclosed the buildings of his chosen home, quietly knocked on the wooden gate, bade farewell to his companions, and entered the haven of his dreams.

The act was not so much a conversion as a conclusion. It was sudden, carrying with it a violent break from his past life. But he was ready—even eager—for the experiences of the monastery. Trained since age six in schools of the church, or schools directly under the church's influence, he was accustomed to think of the church's calling as the highest on earth. Away from home since age fourteen, he had come unconsciously to think of himself as permanently detached from the obligations he owed his family.

But it was no easy task now to write his father. He knew Hans would be heartbroken over the change of plans he had nursed for many years. Heartbroken he was—heartbroken in emotion, and furious in mind and will.

Hans was not one to let the main line of life be broken this easily. He refused to give his permission. Martin pleaded with him. Hans came to see him and found his son immovable. It seemed for many months that the break between them would be severe and permanent. But the plague intervened.

The disease came again to Erfurt in late fall, and rumor drifted up to Mansfield that it had claimed Martin Luther. Poor Hans could not believe it. Meanwhile, he was fearful for the lives of his two younger sons, for the plague had come to Mansfield, too. In middle life, his heart heavy with the defection of Martin, he stood by their bedsides as they died. Crushed by grief, it brought him some relief to be told the report of Martin's death had been false.

Neighbors pleaded that Hans allow God the service of his oldest son. At last he consented, but inwardly he never approved.

Martin rejoiced, although he knew his father was consenting without delight. How Margaret felt we do not know. Probably she thanked God secretly for bestowing His gracious favor on her son.

In the Erfurt monastery, while the home in Mansfield went through the valley of the shadow of death, the newcomer to the Augustinians submitted himself willingly to disciplines of the order. When he knelt for the initial acceptance into the order, he heard the prior* pray over him:

> Lord Jesus Christ, our Leader and our
> Strength, we humbly pray Thee to separate
> Thy servants . . . from carnal conversation
> and from the uncleanness of earthly actions
> by holiness infused in them from on high, and
> pour forth into them the grace by which they
> persevere in Thee.

Hearing this, Luther's mind and heart were fixed on the holy life. Like the prince of Anhalt, seen long ago begging in the streets of Magdeburg, now the master of arts begged bread in the streets of Erfurt. It was not for the sake of bread that he begged, but for the sake of sweet humility.

He was taught how to walk, how to sit at table, how to rise, how to understand the sign language of the daily routine, how to wear his clothes, and how to do all the other little things that make the monastic day an ordered existence. There was no undue severity, only the well-known regimen of the monastery.

---

*The superior of a religious house

The discipline endured. His father's permission granted and his mind at ease, Luther was ready for the final vows by September 1506. In accordance with the ritual of the order, he vowed his life to the service of God in the monastic calling. He was tonsured and received the habit of the order. The long, flowing black robe was put on him. When he knelt before his prior for the taking of the vows, he heard this prayer offered for him:

> Know, Lord Jesus Christ, Thy servant among Thy sheep, that he may know Thee, and denying himself may not follow a strange shepherd, nor hear the voice of strangers, but Thine, who sayest, "Who serveth Me, let him follow Me."

Hans Luther hoped devoutly that the call of God had been real and that the devil had not tricked Martin into a vow he would regret. For his part, Martin was content that the call had been evident and clear.

So his mature years opened with the prospect of vigorous, efficient, satisfying service to the church. His years under his father's control had passed, and he was at the absolute command of his superiors in the "warfare of Christ."

THE WARFARE OF CHRIST
1506-1510

Increasingly, Luther's thoughts turned to the problems of religion. His life in the monastery was moving steadily toward the conquest of fleshly desires. He and his comrades fought persistently against the encroachment of worldly thought. This, his first test in the religious life, called for heroic efforts. He examined his conscience severely and with the relentless honesty that was one of his most outstanding characteristics. Again and again, the desires of the world still found a home in his mind.

The monastic routine was intensified in an effort to bring him the release he so greatly needed. Day after day, in prayer and work, he concentrated on the cleansing of his mind. But the mind does not cleanse easily.

So Luther drove himself still harder. In later years he referred to this experience as his "martyrdom" in the monastery. In fact, he was moving in the accepted paths of the historic church when he bore down upon himself. This was the way the saints trod. He fasted until the hours seemed unreal and strength was so far gone that he could hardly move. In this weakened condition, his thoughts loomed large and intense. In his struggle to understand God, the elements of judgment and fear were uppermost, and there was no one to relieve his terror. He locked himself into his unheated cell and remained there to pray until exhaustion overcame him and his brethren had to break in the door. Before the altar of the monastery church he spent long hours in prayer, to the point of slipping unconscious to the cold floor.

Luther was not being abused by the order. He was following to the extreme the counsels of his order and his church, seeking to know that his life was well-accepted in the sight of God. One does not find this part of Luther in the remarks taken down around the Wittenburg table after 1530, when the great struggle was over and Luther was idolized. But it is seen in the letters written in the early years to Braun and Staupitz.

Luther was a marked man in the order. His fine record in the university was known; his personality was felt throughout Erfurt; and he showed promise of great usefulness when he entered the monastery. His superiors were attentive to him, kind, and gently concerned. They set him to study and destined him to teach theology. His monastic preceptor,* unknown to us by name, was sympathetic and was always loved by Luther.

The deep trouble was not between Luther and his superiors, but within his own mind. On this battleground the protagonists were arrayed against each other.

This inner strife increased as the day approached for his ordination and the saying of his first mass. Luther approached these events with mingled terror and exaltation. He was to know now the sacred hand of the church placed upon his head, setting him apart for the work of salvation. The superiors had instructed him well in the meaning of ordination. He had moved step by step in the custom of the church, becoming subdeacon and deacon, and now was to be made a priest.

In preparing for the ordination, he read Gabriel Biel's *Canon of the Mass*. Staupitz, Luther's vicar-general,† and John Nathin, his teacher, both had studied under Biel. So Luther read the work with a sense of authority. Here he learned of the supreme worth and necessity of the priest, of the tremendous moment when the priest in prayer at the altar "makes the body of Christ" and calls upon God

---

*Tutor

†An administrative deputy (as of a Roman Catholic or Anglican bishop)

to consider the needs of the people. When he thought of himself, Martin Luther, standing before the cross and offering—under the divine law of his church—the Crucified One again to God in propitiation for sin, the idea was almost more than his sensitive spirit could stand. His whole heart went out in love and adoration at the thought of the Mass. But when he turned inward and considered how unworthy he was for such a task, the world seemed to fall in blinding light around him, and his strength failed.

In April 1507, when he was twenty-three, Luther knelt at the feet of his superiors to be made one in the long succession of priests in the western Catholic Church. He was deeply conscious of his high calling and fervent in accepting all the church's major doctrines.

He sang his first Mass on May 2, 1507. The date was set for the convenience of Hans Luther and other friends. Conrad Hutter was invited from Eisenach. In the quiet of his cell, but from the tumult of his heart, Martin wrote to invite his beloved John Braun, vicar of St. Mary's in Eisenach:

Erfurt, April 22, 1507

Greeting in Christ Jesus our Lord. I should fear, most gentle friend, to trouble your kindness by an importunate letter, did I not consider your heartfelt affection for me proved by the many benefits you have conferred upon me. Wherefore, relying on our mutual friendship, I do not hesitate to send this letter, which I am sure will find you attentive and affable.

God, glorious and holy in all His works, has deigned to exalt me, wretched and unworthy sinner, and to call me into His sublime ministry, only for His mercy's sake. I ought to be thankful for the glory of such divine goodness (as much as dust may be) and to fulfil the duty laid upon me.

Wherefore the fathers have set aside the Sunday Cantate (May 2) for my first Mass, God willing. That day I shall celebrate Mass before God for the first time, the day being chosen for the convenience of my father. To this I made bold to invite you, kind friend, but certainly not as though I were doing you any favor deserving the trouble of such a journey, nor that I think my poor and humble self worthy of your coming to me, but because I learned your benevolence and willingness to oblige me when I was recently with you, as I have also at other times. Dearest father, as you are in age and in care for me, master in merit, and brother in religion, if private business will permit you, deign to come and help me with your gracious presence and prayers, that my sacrifice may be acceptable in God's sight. You shall have my kinsman, Conrad, sacristan* of the St. Nicholas Church, or anyone else you wish to accompany you on the way, if you are free from business yourself.

Finally I ask that you come right to the monastery and stay with us a little while (for I do not fear you will settle down here), and do not go to the inn at the cross-roads. For you ought to be a

---

*A church officer in charge of the sacristy (vestry)

celler, that is, the inhabitant of a cell. Farewell in Christ Jesus our Lord.

Brother Martin Luther of Mansfield

P.S.—Those excellent men of the Schalbe Foundation certainly deserve well of me, but I dare not burden them with much asking, for I am persuaded that it would not be suitable to their order and rank for me to invite them to my humble affair, and molest them with the wishes of a monk now dead to the world. Nevertheless I am in doubt whether they would be pleased or annoyed by an invitation. Wherefore kindly do not mention it, but when occasion offers, tell them how grateful I am to them.

It is a letter of special interest. The name and thought of Christ were not far from his mind, since he opened and closed the letter with the familiar phrase. There was no reflection of unhappiness in the monastic life; on the contrary, the letter breathed a certain contentment and joy. There was not revealed any undue harshness from his superiors.

The letter set forth the famous contrast that is always a necessary part of Catholic piety and that undoubtedly was of supreme importance to Luther: "God, glorious and holy in all His works—me, wretched and unworthy sinner." This mighty gulf between God and man has been prominent in the religious thought of the ages, and Luther was apparently sensitive to it from early years.

Many a religious experience followed the recognition of this contrast and the adjustment necessary in the individual's thought.

His Mansfield friends showed no lack of interest. On the appointed day, Hans Luther, now prosperous, rode into Erfurt at the head of twenty horsemen. He presented himself at the monastery, was well received by the monks, and gave them a gift of money large enough to pay for all expenses. They visited and talked until the hour for service, then silently took their places in the church.

Luther had been preparing for this hour for many months, yet it seemed now that his will would fail. The kindly words of a superior just before he entered steadied him some, but hardly enough. At the thought of addressing God personally he was terror stricken: the words almost stopped in his throat, his tongue cleaved to the roof of his mouth, and he felt an almost uncontrollable desire to turn and run from the altar.

Fright mixed with sensitive appreciation took possession of him. The fear arose from the realization of what he was doing. A release from this terror would come later, with a keener sense of the place of the human in the church organization, a maturing attitude toward the observance, a stronger assurance, and a little experience in the technique of priesthood.

But fear was not all. Here was a sincere, devout young man standing for the first time in his life at the height of religious experience. Here was honest, searching appreciation of the act of worship.

Martin Luther stood at the altar of the medieval church with every nerve trembling while the mightiest words known to man came slowly and with difficulty from his lips. Hans Luther bowed his heart in prayer in the cool, silent church and heard the voice of his boy fill the house with the presence of God.

Later, at the table in the refectory, Hans and Martin, who had not seen each other since July 1505, talked over the affairs of life. Hans described the health and activity of Margaret, the growth of the brothers and sisters, and the general condition of the mines and furnaces. He told of the plague in that terrible summer and fall of 1505, of the deaths of Martin's brothers.

Life seemed suddenly serious and quiet then, and the talk turned to Martin. Hans was still unhappy over the "religious" calling. Martin argued that it was the will of God and told again of the divine call that had come to him on the road near Stotterheim.

But Hans was unsure. "God grant that it was not a mere illusion and deception," he said.

This disturbed Martin, but he suggested that his happiness in the cloister was sufficient justification for his action. Hans remained wistful over his broken dreams. He called Martin sharply on his disobedience, saying, while all around the table listened, "Have you not read in Scripture that one shall honor one's father and mother?"

So the conversation ended. Martin never forgot his father's appeal to Scripture, and he felt himself tempted more than once by Hans' suggestion that the vision at Stotterheim could have come from the devil as well as from God.

Hans rode out from the monastery courtyard at the head of his party and started home. Martin returned contentedly to his study and prayer.

Luther's personal religious development paralleled his theological and biblical study in the Erfurt monastery. Here he studied under very highly regarded teachers. The interplay of theological study and personal experience was very definite. During the years when he was deeply troubled by the lack of inner peace, he was studying the theorists of the church. Inevitably, this meant every theory of theology would be tested in his personal experience. By the intensity of that personal experience, he became a religious pragmatist. And the studies brought to the battleground of his personal faith many a worthy protagonist from the fathers of the church, from the scholastics, or from Scripture itself.

The Erfurt monastery took its task of study faithfully, furnishing the teachers for the theological faculty at the university. Under one of them, John Nathin, Luther studied systematically. Nathin was not a particularly good teacher, but he was teaching in the reigning tradition as interpreted by Gabriel Biel. As Luther was influenced by Biel in preparing for the priesthood, so he was influenced by him as he laid the foundation of his philosophic thought.

The Biel tradition gave Luther a distrust of Aristotle, whose principles of logic underlay the major work of the scholastic movement. It also encouraged the development of the critical faculties—something Occam, founder of this philosophic school, had done so sharply. Occam was a Franciscan who had carried to logical completion the implied distrust of the papacy which the Franciscan order had always known. He was openly convinced popes and councils could err. But Biel, Occam's follower, did not admit this, nor did Nathin. So it may have been from Occam, not from Biel or Nathin, that Luther learned to distrust the papacy.

Most important of the influences by Nathin and the philosophers was the conviction that man could attain righteousness by his own will and action. They taught Luther he could rely on stern, rigorous thinking and decisive, ordered action to produce a sense of assurance in his life. So Luther went from study to prayer to action, striving to find the peace of God. Yet all the while, he knew the immovable righteousness of God which he, in his humble human life, was utterly unable to gain.

He found a hopeful, happy counterbalance in biblical studies. The rules of the Augustinian order required it, and Luther was given a red-bound Bible for his personal use when he entered the order. This book was precious to him. He read it so steadily and thoroughly that he could quote whole passages by heart. Biblical content became the major unit in his thinking, and he used it as a criterion for all judgments.

One of his teachers, Dr. Usingen, disturbed by Luther's constant intellectual activity, advised him to let the Bible alone. "What is the Bible?" Usingen asked. "It is better to read the old doctors who have drawn the truth from the Bible. The Bible is the cause of all sedition. . . ."

It has been said that Nathin once forbade Luther to read the Bible. Nathin must have been exasperated often by the biblical quotations his student could use. But the vicar-general was more understanding and revoked the prohibition.

The medieval church had ample cause to beware the independent study of Scripture, for this was the food of heresy as well as that of the lovely piety of a Bernard or a Francis. History bears witness to the exceptional strength of Scripture to make men think and act along independent lines.

Luther immersed himself in the Bible at Erfurt. He read it long and carefully, grounding himself in it with intense, imaginative eagerness. What came later to public expression in his lectures at the University of Wittenberg had its beginnings here. His mind and heart found great refreshment in the exhaustless well. The Christ in the Gospels and the Christ in the letters of Paul began slowly to supplant in Luther's mind the Christ of stern, severe judgment.

But it is no wonder he found his mind in constant upheaval, turning from philosophy to Scripture and back to philosophy again. One taught him to counter his sense of insufficiency with more strident efforts of the will and action; the other taught the open acceptance of the free love of God, unearned and undeserved, but real and historic in Christ.

His study broadened now, and in the fathers of the church he began to find the central stream of piety, the source of assurance other men had possessed. He longed for the sense that he was God's. The great insatiable desire of Christianity for the perfect life was upon him. He was not at war with gross temptation and the life of the flesh, in open defiance of God's commands. This struggle was within the mind. The stark reality of Jesus' requirement that the mind be pure terrified him. There were fewer obstacles to God's commandments within the monastic life, but Luther's elemental honesty refused to let the cry of his conscience be stilled.

In the sacrament of penance he hoped to find relief. But

the beauty of this sacrament lies in the heart's belief in God's forgiving goodness. Thus the sacrament becomes an expression, not a contributing cause. And Luther did not believe.

He argued it out with his confessor, holding that God necessarily must be angry at him for his sins. The gentler, older man told him to go read his Apostles' Creed again. There he would find the commandment to believe in the "forgiveness of sins." He finally told Luther point-blank, "It is not God Who is angry with you. It is you who are angry with God."

The confessor told Luther to read the works of Bernard of Clairvaux, who found the grace of God to be the source of peace. So Luther sat in his cell in Erfurt, and the centuries disappeared while Bernard spoke to him. He told Luther of the surpassing sweetness of the historic Christ and led Luther into a vision of the crucifixion from which the riches of the love of God could be understood. We can begin to feel a little of the exaltation that came to Luther in his need when we sing:

> O sacred Head, now wounded,
>> With grief and shame weighed down;
> Now scornfully surrounded
>> With thorns, thine only crown;
> O Sacred Head, what glory,
>> What bliss till now was Thine!
> Yet, though despised and gory,
>> I joy to call Thee mine.
>
> What language shall I borrow
>> To thank Thee, dearest Friend,

For this Thy dying sorrow,
  Thy pity without end?
O make me Thine forever;
  And should I fainting be,
Lord, let me never, never,
  Outlive my love for Thee.
Be near me when I am dying,
  O show Thy cross to me;
And for my succor flying,
  Come, Lord, to set me free:
These eyes, new faith receiving,
  From Jesus shall not move;
For he who dies believing
  Dies safely, through Thy love.

Surrounded by a mood like the one suggested in the hymn, Luther felt the hold of sin weakening, the dread of death lessening. Bernard, too, had felt the strong sense of sin, and he, too, had fled the world to make in the monastic life the mighty effort for redemption.

The winters passed over Luther's head and the sense of sin remained within him, but in the historic work of Christ he found the proof of God's everlasting affection. Around Christ and the crucifixion, then, he wove his hope. All the operations of the visible, established church, which he loved dearly, became avenues of the grace of God. So Luther, understanding Bernard, found the way a little easier and the nearness of God a little more discernible.

Eager in his studies, Luther turned to Augustine, whose name his order bore. The magic of this name was everywhere, and Luther read his works to learn what he knew of the way to God. The very books Luther used can be seen today, and the notes Luther entered in the margins show the movement of his mind.

The issues that confronted Luther were issues of personal religion, but the solutions were sought in the realms of systematic thought. The combination of these two realms is more apparent in Augustine than in any of the great church fathers, for he was, to a greater degree, the product of his own religious experience. Only grace could have rescued him from the depths of depravity to which he had sunk; thus grace occupied his thoughts. Sin was central in his teachings because he knew it personally. Grace was irresistible because he himself could not resist it. He taught that the human will is impotent, because his was impotent.

When he turned to Scripture for confirmation of these concepts, he found it. His sinful nature found its cause in Adam. His doctrine of the enslaved was affirmed by Paul. Supremely important, his Christ of faith and experience became the great liberating agent of the whole scriptural story; metaphysics clothed the humble human experience with dignity.

It was with growing satisfaction that Luther read the pages of St. Augustine. No father of the church could speak more directly and more strongly on the very points where he felt himself lost. The difficulties of his speculative thought began to disappear in the presence of Augustine's piety. A strong and new conception of Christ began slowly to establish itself in his heart.

"To believe is to believe in his humanity which is given for us in this life for life and salvation. For He, himself, through our faith in his Incarnation is our life, our justification, and our resurrection." This is in Luther's handwriting on the margin of a page of Augustine's essay on the Trinity.

Luther's return to Augustine's point of view was not made alone. The very advice of his superiors to read Augustine is evidence of the general acceptability of the great African father. Membership in the Augustine order carries with it a special interest in Augustine. Historian Albert Ritschl also maintains that there was at the end of the fifteenth Century a general return to the fundamental position of Augustine on exclusive grace, and that this return went hand in hand with the general breakdown of the Occamist philosophy, which had supported monk righteousness, in which Luther found himself struggling.

Thus Luther appropriated the best tradition of thought to which he was heir.

Luther was greatly troubled by the spectre of eternal damnation involved in the doctrine of predestination. In Augustine, he had the chance to study the master of that doctrine, who was at the same time the master of the doctrine of God's free grace in Christ. So predestination lost its terror and passed into the larger doctrine of human dependence on the will of God. It became a truly pious consideration. Its solution was offered in Christ simultaneously with its damnation in Adam. Luther's pent-up feelings on the harassing subject of predestination, under which he felt himself damned, found release and comfort in the thought of Christ. Augustine was indeed a rock in a weary land, and Luther temporarily rested.

No modern historian has a better right to pass judgment on the effect of Augustine upon Luther than Adolf

Harnack, a master in Augustinian and Lutheran studies. He noted:

> Augustine was the theologian of the ancient Church who had taught that God works his "Will and Consummation" in us, that Faith, Hope, and Love are gifts of His Grace, and that God joins with us in every effort for good; on this we shall place complete faith. As Luther read this the temptations began to be less frequent—he did not experience a sudden liberation and assurance of God, but gradually he came out of his doubt and extreme anxiety. And this is to be noted: Peace came first into his heart, the confidence of the soul before the insight of the mind.

The ritual of the church also began to yield up to Luther its hidden spirit. In service after service of the appointed monastic round, he heard the historic affirmations of the reliance of the church on Christ's mercies. He chanted the great liturgical praises to Jesus as the hope and salvation of the world.

He did not always transfer the strength and beauty of these forms of worship into his own life. He had difficulty giving the "praises" a living reality. No matter how lovely the liturgy was in theory, Luther received it under the aspect of his own environment. The men around him were more real interpreters of the faith than was the liturgy they chanted. The theoretical position of the church was available for normal purposes only in the personal interpretation and emphasis it received from its local representatives. Luther had to struggle through the interpretations to the essence. Only when he got into the thick of study and personal guidance did his thought begin to clarify; then it outstripped its local time period in its return to the older Augustinian position.

When the great religious experiences have been encased in a beautiful form and become daily liturgy, they invariably have lost their power. That is partly because Luther and the others who have traveled this path too often expect the repetition of the great phrases and the careful attention to liturgy to bring the reward to the heart. But each must find for himself this pearl of great price. The halting logic of one's own heart is superior at times to the mighty eloquence of the church.

Nevertheless, the liturgical service of the church and monastery brought into Luther's mind many of the ideas about Jesus that finally came to fruition in an adjusted theological structure and a transformed faith.

The man most influential in Luther's development was John von Staupitz. He had entered the university at Leipzig in 1485, received his M.A. at Tubingen, and lectured there in theology. He joined the Augustinian order and was chosen vicar of the Saxon province in 1503, two years before Luther entered. When the elector Frederick established the University of Wittenberg, Staupitz was made dean of the theological faculty. So Luther first knew him as vicar-general and professor in the neighboring school.

Staupitz, visiting the Erfurt monastery, became interested in the young monk who had so suddenly left the university for the cloister. He watched Luther's inner spiritual struggle, which was reflected so thoroughly in his external appearance. Luther had come to the monastery a strong, enthusiastic young man of twenty-two, and Staupitz watched him grow thin, tired, and nervous.

Eager to help and conserve this brilliant new member of the order, Staupitz befriended him. As the first two severe years went by, Luther began to feel that in Staupitz he had a sympathetic, understanding superior. Time after time he unburdened his soul to Staupitz. He revealed how he had feared eternal damnation, how the doctrine of predestination worried him, how he was unconvinced he had won the mercy of Christ. The advice of Staupitz was always gentle and to the point. With keen insight he tried to make Luther see the introspective quality of his meditation and to direct him to historic and actual things.

One day Staupitz said, "Look not on your own imaginary sins, but look at Christ crucified, where your real sins are forgiven, and hold with deep courage to God." Luther never forgot this. Throughout his life he acknowledged his indebtedness to Staupitz for teaching him to center the conception of forgiveness around the crucifixion of Christ.

They spent many hours together, and the older man grew increasingly fond of the younger. He knew Luther's restless, sensitive spirit needed constant work, and he recognized the fine quality of his mind.

It was not entirely a surprise, then, when in 1508 Staupitz moved Luther from the Erfurt monastery to the one at Wittenberg. Luther was ready for active work. The change came suddenly, and he found himself at Wittenberg with hardly an opportunity to bid good-bye to his old friends.

He wrote again to John Braun, remembering, as always, in the major movements of his life, this friend from his school days who had done so much toward his religious calling.

Wittenberg, March 17, 1509
Brother Martin Luther sends you greeting and wishes you salvation and the Saviour Himself, Jesus Christ.

Cease, master and father, even more loved than revered, cease, I pray, to wonder, as you have been doing, that I left you secretly and silently, or at least would have so left you, were there not still a tie between us, or as if the power of ingratitude, like a north wind, had chilled our love and wiped the memory of your kindness from my heart. Indeed, no! I have not acted thus, or rather I meant not to act thus, although I may have been forced to act so as unintentionally to give you occasion to think evil of me.

I went, I confess, and yet I did not go, but left my greater and better part with you still. I can only persuade you that this is so by your own faith in me. As you conceived in of your own kindness and favor only, I hope you will never suffer it to be slain or diminished without my fault, as you have never done before. So I have gone farther from you in body but come nearer to you in mind, provided you are not unwilling, which I hope you are not at all.

To come to the point, that I be not longer compelled to suspect that your friendship doubts my constancy (would that the suspicion were false!) behold how hard I have tried to steal this time from my many and various affairs to write you, especially as messengers are scarce, and were they plentiful, could rarely be used on account of their ignorance and carelessness. My only purpose in writing is to commend myself to you, and to express my hope that you will continue to think of me as you would wish to have me think of you. Although I cannot be, and do not think I am, equal to you in any good thing, nevertheless I have a great affection for you which I cannot give you now as I have so often given it to you in the past. I know that your generous spirit expects nothing from me save the things of the spirit, that is, to have the same knowledge of the Lord, and one heart and soul as we have one faith in him.

Wonder not that I departed without saying farewell. For my departure was so sudden that it was almost unknown to my fellow-monks. I wished to write you but had time and leisure for nothing except to regret that I had to break away without saying good-by.

Now I am at Wittenberg, by God's command or permission. If you wish to know my condition, I am well, thank God, except that my studies are very severe, especially philosophy, which from the first I would willingly have changed for theology; I mean that theology which searches out the meat of the nut, and the kernel of the grain, and the marrow of the bones. But God is God; man often,

*if not always, is at fault in his judgment. He is
our God, He will sweetly govern us forever.*

*Please deign to accept this, which has been set
down in haste and extemporally, and if you can
get any messengers to me let me have a share of
your letters. I shall try to do the same for you in
return. Farewell in the beginning and the end,
and believe me such as you wish me. Again
farewell.*

Brother Martin Luther, Augustinian

He was definitely committed now to biblical studies,
chafing under the philosophical emphasis. The whole
desire of his life focused more and more around the
Bible. He could not teach it, however, until he had
earned his doctor's degree. He therefore was lecturing on
Aristotle's ethics, scholastic philosophy having been his
major study at Erfurt.

On March 9, 1509, he took his first degree in theology
at the University of Wittenberg. Staupitz now insisted
that Luther continue studying for his doctorate in theology so he could become a professor on the theological
faculty.

Staupitz said to him one day, half-seriously, half-jokingly, "You should take the degree of doctor so as to
have something to do."

Luther protested that his strength was already used up
in his regular duties and that he was sure he could not
survive the duties of a professorship.

Staupitz answered, "Do you not know that the Lord has
a great deal of business to attend to in which He needs the

assistance of clever people? If you should die you might be His counselor."

Luther laughed and agreed to follow Staupitz's advice, taking up his studies for the doctorate.

In preparation for lecturing on the Bible, the university required that the candidate teach for three semesters the Sentences of Peter Lombard. This standard textbook in theological instruction was written at Paris, where Peter was made bishop in 1159. For this work Luther returned to Erfurt. An entry in the books of Wittenberg University states that he was sent back to Erfurt in the fall of 1509 "because he had not satisfied the Wittenberg faculty." Luther added the note, "because he had no means to; Erfurt must pay." He began his work under Staupitz's supervision, and they kept in close touch.

The text of the *Sentences* from which Luther lectured is known, as are his marginal notes. He was not unfriendly to the author's thinking, but it is interesting to note the deficiency he perceived in Lombard. "He would have been a great man," Luther said years later, "if he had read more in the Bible and incorporated it in his writings."

The notes Luther made that winter indicate vast reading. Occam, D'Ailly, Biel, Bernard, Augustine, Scotus, Chrysostom, Jerome, Ambrose, and Hilary are all referenced, but his beloved Scripture is quoted most often.

He continually emphasized faith against reason, tradition against speculation, theology against philosophy. He evidenced a keen consciousness of the power of sin, and tended to bring every problem around the person of Jesus. Luther expressly asserted that Christ, not "wisdom," was the first creation. Christ—the "son of God" and "our Redeemer"—was the center of Luther's reflection on sin.

Robert H. Fife, in a study called *Young Luther*, concluded a very good examination of the notes on Lombard:

> The framework of the marginal notes on
> Lombard is, then, the ancient and traditional
> structure, but there is growing within the
> frame a spirit of trust in the grace of God and
> of reliance on the Holy Scriptures which
> shows that the soul struggles of the young
> monk have not been in vain.

It is not clear by any means that Luther took a new position during or before these lectures, but it is clear that some of the elements necessary to a new position found expression. Sin and grace were evidently the centers of thought. Christ was receiving some of the adjectives and descriptive phrases which show Him as the way by which sin is overcome and forgiven, and grace is received.

There were strength and independence of thought in the notes. Luther was growing, was becoming master of his own mind, and was ready for increased responsibilities.

three

Journeys

HAIL, HOLY ROME!
1510-1511

THE EXPERIENCES OF Erfurt in this second residence were broken by the great opportunity to visit Rome. It is a tribute to the position Luther already had attained within the order that, when a dispute necessitated representation at Rome, Luther was chosen to accompany the messenger sent by the order to the Papal See.

Staupitz was, of course, involved in the difficulty. It was an administrative problem; a minority group in the order was protesting a decision of the vicar-general. So it was a great comfort to Staupitz that Martin Luther was the second member of the commission.

In October 1510, John von Mecheln and Martin Luther left Erfurt on their long walk to Rome. Insofar as possible, they were to spend the nights in friendly cloisters. It was the custom of the men of the order when journeying to walk silently, one behind the other.

Down through the lovely valleys of central Germany Luther and Mecheln walked. Luther's boyhood years had been filled with an appreciation of natural beauty, and it must have been a strange and lovely release to find himself on the open road. In boyhood, in peasant costume he had roamed the hills of Mansfield. In school days he often had journeyed in student costume between Mansfield, Eisenach, and Erfurt. Now, in the black robes of the Augustinian order, he was out on the high road again.

The long discipline of the monastic life had changed him considerably. Gone was the quick, elastic, joyous step of his late boyhood. Yet as the days passed, he found the strength of youth returning to him. He carried in his heart and mind the great soul struggles that were his all-absorbing passion, but he also was breathing the open air. With his books and study far behind, he saw the lovely hills of southern Germany. Journeying over the Alps, he felt the awe those majestic mountains always have inspired.

Descending through the rich plains of northern Italy, the brothers came to Florence. A quarter of a century past the height of its Renaissance, it still possessed rich treasures unsurpassed in the world of art. Raphael, Leonardo da Vinci, Michelangelo, and many other creative geniuses worked in Italy.

But Luther's attention was elsewhere. Oblivious to Florence's beauty in stone and on canvas, he visited the hospitals and churches of the city. Long years afterward he described in detail the fine work of the Florentines in their hospitals. He remembered their cleanliness, efficiency, courtesy, and intelligence. Meanwhile, Michelangelo's godlike *David* was standing in the city square of Florence, but there is no record of Luther's response to it.

He heard with amazement stories of the papal court at Rome and saw at Florence the lives of churchmen of such quality as to shock his quick consciousness of sin. He felt through the spiritual atmosphere of Florence the tremendous memory of Savonarola. The monks he visited in the city told him of those terrible experiences just twelve and one-half years ago when the great Dominican, his conscience weakened under torture, reasserted his real convictions and was hanged and burned in the public square. Luther's mind was filled with the mood of the courageous monk who had morally defied a sinful church.

From Florence down toward Rome the brothers journeyed, through the lovely fields and under the quiet skies of Umbria. They passed towns blessed by the presence of Francis of Assisi and churches immortalized by the works of Giotto.

The night before they arrived in sight of the holy city, behind the hills that separated Rome from the north, Luther's religious devotion rose to almost ecstatic heights. He believed thoroughly in the remission of sins that he should win at the holy places in the city of his faith. His mind was fastened on the great traditions of his fathers in Christian history.

The next day, as he came over the top of Mt. Mario, he saw spread out before him the central city of western Christendom. Overcome with joy, he fell on his knees and cried, "Hail, Holy Rome! Thrice blessed in the blood of the martyrs!" With high expectation he followed John Mecheln through the gate and walked at last within the sacred city.

They lodged in a monastery, where they were treated with kindness. But here they were severely shocked at the indifference and ease with which the monks went through their routine services.

Pope Julius was away from Rome on a campaign against Bologna. The future Pope Leo X, now Cardinal Medici, was at the head of a papal army attacking his native city, Florence. So John von Mecheln carried his papers to the cardinal secretary of state.

Luther was a real pilgrim. He anxiously and joyously sought the great church shrines. He visited the catacombs, recently rediscovered and the object of great interest, and felt the strange influence that comes from the memories of the martyrs buried there. All his religious quest focused itself on the desire to win release from sin's terror. He visited the shrines not only for the sake of his own soul, but for the souls of his family and friends. He was even tempted to wish his father and mother were dead, so that his prayers might release them from purgatory. For his grandfather, long since dead, he could perform this incomparable service.

He went, as was the custom with Roman pilgrims, to the great sacred stairs. Up near the Lateran Church, the real mother church of Roman Catholicism, these stairs were set, leading to a room containing relics of the saints. Roman tradition told Luther the steps were those up which Jesus had walked the night He appeared before Pilate. Pope Leo IV had granted an indulgence of nine years for every step, and there were twenty-eight steps. For centuries the devout in the Catholic faith have climbed these steps, with the proper prayers in their hearts and on their lips, believing in the benefits their church offered for this action. Luther was among them in this belief. He had walked the great pathway of penitence for five years now, and this was a kind of climax.

Yet all the while he had walked the way of penitence, another way had been appearing to him as superior. He had read of it many times in the Bible, in Bernard, in Augustine, and Staupitz had pointed it out to him. Seventy-two years after Luther climbed as a penitent these stairs, his son Paul said he had heard his father tell how in the midst of the climb he recalled the text, "The just shall live by faith," and walked back down.

This story, which Paul heard at eleven years of age and carried in his memory for thirty-eight years, is the sole foundation we have for this recurring tradition of Luther. It might well be true. Luther had read the great Pauline testimony to faith. Bernard and Augustine had died in the pure faith and told Luther so. Staupitz and others had pointed him that way, and the whole trend of his purest Catholic tradition was to turn to the prayers of faith and away from the superstitious confidence in "good works." His mind was keen. He had studied these things intently for years, and he well may have felt the hollowness of this action—especially in view of the impossibility that these steps were true relics.

But the reflection of this event in a sermon long afterward gives a truer picture than does Paul Luther's memory. Preaching in Wittenberg the year before his death, Martin told of some experiences in Rome and related how, as he had reached the top of the stairs, a doubt regarding the power of the practice had come into his mind. "Who knows whether this be true?" he had thought.

Luther did not come down from these steps a rebel

against his church. He did not orient his thinking from this moment around the text, "The just shall live by faith." He did not forsake the great comforts and assurances of his church's sacraments and "works." His mind and soul were forming themselves in tremendous, moving experiences. The "Holy Steps" were not crucial but were only one more movement in the experience. He was a child of Rome when he came, and he was a child of Rome when he left.

But the Rome of Luther's dreams and ideal was broken and forever shattered. The Rome of the apostles, so precious in his mind, became the Rome of reality. He was seeing what was left of Christian Rome when Nicholas V, Calixtus III, Pius II, Paul II, Sixtus IV, Innocent VII, Alexander VI, Pius III, and Julius II were through.

The Renaissance papacy, which had controlled Rome since 1447, with the accession of Nicholas V, had steadily centered its policy around the secularization of the church. Without any leadership from the popes, the moral life of Rome had degenerated steadily. With each of these popes setting an example that defied every one of the Ten Commandments, Rome had become a place of notorious anti-Christian life.

Instead of observing the vows of chastity, Innocent VIII had seen his own daughter married in a hall of the Vatican Palace and sat at the wedding banquet in company with his mistress. In place of the spiritual insight the church should have found in its leader, Alexander VI had given it a powerful, worldly dictatorship. The whole family of the Borgias, Calixtus III, Alexander VI, Cesare, and Lucrezia, had marked Rome with such scandal and immoderate living that the church seemed unable to recover. Rodrigo Borgia had died—of poison, they said—just seven years before Luther's visit.

Pius III, elected because he was a sick man, had lived only a month. Now Julius II, after seven years in office, was at the height of his reign. For him Raphael was painting in the Vatican, working the very month Luther was in Rome. The year before this, Raphael had finished the *Disputa*, symbolizing the truth of the doctrine of "transubstantiation." It shows the concurrent judgment of heaven and Rome. Michelangelo at the moment was chasing his patron Julius to Bologna, leaving the half-finished ceiling and walls of the Sistine Chapel. For Julius, too, Michelangelo was to carve his great *Moses*. But in Julius no vestige of the moral grandeur of Moses could be found.

Luther saw and felt a Rome utterly abandoned to money, luxury, and kindred evils. He was stunned and unable to understand it—but he did not stay in Rome long enough to rebel against it. Four or five weeks at most, and he had to start his journey northward again. One cannot hear scandal enough in four or five weeks or see sufficient evil in that length of time to unseat a devotion held since birth.

Yet as the years went by for Luther and as other things in theology and church organization became clear to him, he remembered the Rome of his visit and could see far more clearly how utterly corrupt was the leadership offered to the great church in 1510.

Reminiscences of the visit occur steadily throughout the *Table Talk*, and this is what was in his mind when, in later years, he thought of Rome:

Rome is a harlot. I would not take a thousand gulden not to have seen it, for I never would have believed the true state of affairs from what other people told me had I not seen it myself. The Italians mocked us for being pious monks, for they hold Christians fools. They say six or seven masses in the time it takes me to say one, for they take money for it and I do not. The only crime in Italy is poverty. They still punish homicide and theft a little, for they have to, but no other sin is too gross for them. . . . So great and bold is Roman impiety that neither God nor man, neither sin nor shame, is feared. All good men who have seen Rome bear witness to this; all bad ones come back worse than before.

In January 1511, the weary Luther, his mind filled with conflicting thoughts, started home with John von Mecheln. Once again he found himself walking through central northern Italy to Milan. Here he found to his amazement a group of priests refusing allegiance to Rome, saying they stood in the succession of the famous Ambrose, Bishop of Milan in the early fourth century.

Here, too, throughout this winter, Leonardo da Vinci, now fifty-eight, was working. The exquisite *Last Supper* was in formation, and Leonardo's genius was moving rapidly through the creative arts.

Northward and over the Alps into his own German lands Luther walked. Some time in February the brothers entered Erfurt.

Luther was glad to pick up his books and the routine of his study again. But life was not the same to him. He had been to Rome. In the journey he had gained some confidence, some assurance, some command of himself which in the days of steady introspection he had never known.

Now Rome would hear from him.

THE RISING TIDE
1511-1516

Luther resumed his work in the Erfurt monastery, teaching there until Staupitz called him again to Wittenberg in the autumn of 1511. Wittenberg was now to be his home until his death.

It was a small, humble town. The 356 houses provided homes for some 3,000 people. The Elbe River, upon which Wittenberg is situated, is at this point shallow and slow moving. No commerce of any kind is possible on it. The soil of the countryside is sandy and poor. The entire area is flat and uninviting. The townspeople were uneducated, coarse, and generally uncultured.

The town had two churches. The cathedral church attached to the university was supported by the elector, who filled it with relics. A smaller, less conspicuous parish church served the inhabitants of the town. The Augustinian monks owned a cloister there, known as the "Black Cloister" because of the black robes they always wore. Luther came to this cloister.

His duties the first year of his Wittenberg residence were mainly personal study. He was following the plans laid by himself and Staupitz for his doctor's degree, preparing for the professorship in biblical interpretation. Throughout the first year he prepared himself for his examinations. But his life was varied, and he found himself deeply interested in the affairs of his order.

His mission to Rome the previous year had been only the beginning of a rise to recognition from his brother monks. In May 1512 he and Staupitz journeyed to Cologne to attend the district meeting. Here Luther was elected subprior of the Wittenberg monastery. On his return from Cologne he assumed many administrative functions under the prior.

On October 18, 1512, he received the doctor of theology degree. Elector Frederick, apparently at the request of Staupitz, paid the usual fee for the promotion—fifty gulden. The receipt Luther signed for the money still exists.

He wrote to invite his friends from Erfurt to come up for his promotion, but relations now were strained between Luther and the Erfurt superiors. The Erfurt men, particularly his teacher Nathin, resented very much his transfer to Wittenberg. They thought he was breaking one of the major obligations of university honor by taking his degree at Wittenberg instead of Erfurt. In the opening sentence of his letter Luther stated the cause of his Wittenberg residence as the command of his superiors. Nevertheless, from this day there was to be an increasing difference between Luther and the Erfurt teaching tradition. He steadily stressed the biblical aspect of theology, in opposition to the philosophical bias at Erfurt. The Erfurt men did not come to Wittenberg.

Six days after receiving his doctor's degree, he was

admitted to the university senate, which finally gave him full rights in the teaching profession. He accepted these obligations with his usual intensity and sincerity. He believed the church had set him apart to teach, and to this he was bound. He felt an apostolic authority lay behind his work of exposition.

When Wittenberg—only nine years old as a university—admitted Martin Luther to its staff of professors, it placed itself in line for leadership of all the universities of western Europe. Strong men already on the faculty, such as Nicholas Armsdorf and Andrew Bodenstein (known to history as Carlstadt), soon succumbed to the intellectual leadership and moral vigor of their new colleague. Around Luther there grew a Wittenberg tradition, so that within a few years men began to speak of "the Wittenberg theology."

Sometime during this year of 1512-13, Luther for the first time focused his conflicting thoughts and saw them temporarily in such clarity and harmony that he called this experience the "birthday" of his faith. In the tower of the Black Cloister, where he often studied, he kept his attention on the great text in Romans 1:17: "The just shall live by faith."

The whole problem of his life, since he first felt the call of religion in boyhood, was the problem of sin and the acceptance of his life in the sight of God. He believed so thoroughly in the perfect righteousness and perfect justice of God and felt so thoroughly his own sinfulness that he could not understand how anyone could be justified in the sight of God.

What, then, did Paul mean when he wrote, "The just shall live by faith?" Paul, above all other men, had pointed out the sinfulness of the human race. Paul had cried out, as Luther so often cried out, "O wretched man that I am! who shall deliver me from the body of this death?" Paul had talked of the warfare between flesh and spirit. Paul had believed in the immovable and eternal will of God operating in human life.

Luther's mind marshaled to its task the positions of Bernard and Augustine, and he remembered the constant advice of Staupitz to look upon the crucifixion. He recalled how in countless places Paul had centered his whole thought around the crucifixion. By belief in the crucifixion, could Luther find release from this burden of sinfulness? Was it, then, by faith in the historic work of Christ? Paul must have meant by "faith" the acceptance of the work of Christ! He must have meant that God had, through Christ, wrought a justification of sinful men who would open their lives to the Word!

Could even he, then, Martin Luther, by the sheer act of acceptance of the historic work of Christ, find that mighty gulf between himself and God bridged? Was it true that God's righteousness was not the righteousness of condemnation but the righteousness transferred from Christ to him?

He then could feel the mighty rhythm of Pauline thought, wherein his sinfulness was ever present, yet God's justification, likewise, was ever present. Inwardly he felt the ancient, pure strength so well known to Pauline Christians. It was now no longer a battle with God to force God's recognition of his good deeds, for God was on his side. He saw, as it were, in one great vision, all the tremendous movement in the human race, from its sin in Adam to its redemption in Christ. He, Martin

Luther, could stand steadfast by faith in Christ and know that the tremendous pressure of his sin was offset by the endless mercy made possible in Christ.

This was the hour of his freedom, the hour of his great "illumination." From this day forth there was a new note in his message. All his teachings began, centered, and ended in the history of redemption.

He came from the tower room not with his whole theology clearly wrought, but with its basis fixed. He faced the first years of his biblical lecturing secure in the conviction that he had found the key to understanding the Scriptures. Through all the wars into which his life carried him, he held steadfast to his understanding that "the just shall live by faith." It was not that faith moved without works, but that life came by faith, and works were the result.

He lectured in the university from 1513 to 1515 on the Psalms. His method was to have a copy of the psalm on his desk before him. The copy he used had been printed a month before he began to lecture. It had wide spaces between the printed lines. Luther wrote his comments and notes between the lines. These notes still can be read.

His heart had been troubled for many years over the mighty problems of religious peace. Now his students heard, as though listening to an autobiography, all the tremendous spiritual depth of the Psalms come to life. He lectured in Latin. If his Latin came to him with too much stereotyped scholastic form, he would break into German. His notes show the language changing in midsentence.

When the old forms of university lectures were insufficient to hold the fulness of his message, he created new and striking illustrations. For example, "As the meadow is to the cow, the house to the man, and the nest to the bird, the rock to the chamois, and the stream to the fish, so is the Holy Scripture to the believing soul." When Luther spoke to his students on a particular psalm, they could feel that they were listening to one who spoke with authority, and they flocked to his classroom. "We students heard him gladly, for he spoke to us in our mother-tongue," wrote one of his scholars.

In 1515-16 he lectured on Paul's Epistle to the Romans. This was his own great document, and as he set forth before his students the mind of Paul through chapter after chapter of this book, they saw once again the whole drama of heavenly redemption unveiled before them.

Just before he began his lectures on the ninth chapter of Romans, Erasmus' edition of the Greek New Testament came into his hands, and from that point on it was his lecture book. Erasmus provided fine Greek and Latin helps. Also, though unskilled in its use, Luther kept the Hebrew grammar and lexicon of Reuchlin always on his desk. He strove to bring to Old and New Testament alike the finest aids scholarship could give him.

Here, in the lectures on Psalms and Romans, his conception of theology was formulated systematically. Although his interest was never in the system, as such, but always in practical piety, in these lectures he brought his thoughts into ordered shape. He was jubilant as he found, month after month, all the great problems of his life falling into relation with each other around his acceptance of the historic—not speculative—basis for Christian thought.

As he lectured on Romans, he brought before the

judgment bar of this mighty book the society of his day. He bitterly attacked Julius II and the frightful immorality of Rome. He denounced the governing Curia and all the church hierarchy for their widespread corruption and vileness. Luxury and avarice, pride and selfishness were rampant in the pope's city. Romans 13:13, a text that had brought home its terrible lesson to the unconverted Augustine, now gave Luther a vocabulary for describing Rome: "rioting . . . drunkenness . . . chambering . . . wantonness . . . strife . . . envying." And he begged his generation to heed the glorious exhortation of verse 14: "Put ye on the Lord Jesus Christ, and make not provision for the flesh, to fulfil the lusts thereof." In severe language he arraigned the clergy for thinking their task was to defend the church instead of to preach the Gospel.

He had said to Staupitz a few years earlier that he could not survive the duties of the doctorate many months. But he found to his amazement that strength was added to strength as his life organized itself in his new field. Staupitz had known the caliber of Luther and now saw with great joy the steady progress of the teacher.

In 1516, while these lectures were being given, he published his first book. He had discovered the works of Tauler and the great German mystics. He was so enthusiastic over the little book *A German Theology* that he edited it, saying in the preface that there was no better book after the Bible and Augustine where one could learn the nature of "God, Christ, man, and all things."

The influence of this mystic school in German thought softened Luther considerably in his inner piety. He never became a thorough adherent of the mystic school, for his interests were too practical. But the contribution of the quiet, passive acceptance of the will of God—the central thought of the German mystics—brought to him in these days of inner turmoil a blessed peace.

Luther's days at Wittenberg were not confined to the professorship. His elevation to the doctor's degree involved preaching to his brother monks. He had objected steadfastly to this in the early years, looking forward to it with fear and trembling. He argued the case with Staupitz, describing his fear. Staupitz said he, too, had been afraid of preaching in his early days, but the fear had vanished.

So Luther began, at first preaching only to the monks in their little wooden chapel, 20 x 30 feet, attached to the cloister. Here his sermons developed a distinctive quality and attracted such attention that the town council of Wittenberg petitioned him to preach in the parish church. So he took up the duties of parish preacher.

The earliest sermon extant is one he preached, in all probability, in 1514. His text was, "Whatsoever ye would that men should do to you, do you even so to them." The sermon showed what was to be the major quality of his preaching. He talked simply and straightforwardly. He named the areas of life in which his hearers lived, talked about things they knew daily, analyzed them in the light of Christian principles, and exhorted his people to walk in Christian ways.

Added to the burdens of the professorship and preaching came Luther's election in May 1515, at the district meeting of the Order at Gotha, as district vicar of the monasteries in Meissen and Thuringe. There were ten monasteries in the district when he first was elected, with the addition later of Eisleben, the town of his birth.

He was required, by the rules of his office, to visit each of these monasteries once a year. Each visit naturally involved time and effort.

His correspondence increased tremendously with this new responsibility. He found all the hours of his day filled with important tasks. He had to preach to monk and villager. He had not only to lecture, but to lecture with intensity and intelligence, for he was already the acknowledged leader in a new movement. He had to exercise discipline in his administration over distant monasteries. He ceased to be the introspective, troubled monk of the Erfurt days, becoming a strong, assured, confident leader, enjoying the respect and confidence of his entire circle.

Yet humility, genuineness, and deep piety remained the root characteristics of his life. He possessed that strangely fascinating characteristic of being so humble in personal thought that he lost himself completely in public action and professional responsibility. He was a tireless worker. He saw the detail of his many tasks clearly and kept a personal understanding of the problems that confronted him.

The quality of the true Christian administrator shines beautifully in a letter he wrote to one of the monasteries regarding a brother who required discipline:

To John Bercken,
Augustinian Prior at Mayence

Dresden, May 1, 1516

Greeting in the Lord! Reverend and excellent

Father Prior! I am grieved to learn that there is with your Reverence one of my brothers, a certain George Baumgartner, of our convent at Dresden, and that, alas! he sought refuge with you in a shameful manner, and for a shameful cause. I thank your faith and your duty for receiving him and thus bringing his shame to an end. That lost sheep is mine, he belongs to me; it is mine to seek him, and, if it please the Lord Jesus, to bring him back. Wherefore I pray your reverence by our common faith in Christ and by our common Augustinian vow, to send him to me in dutiful charity either at Dresden or at Wittenberg, or rather to persuade him lovingly and gently to come of his own accord. I shall receive him with open arms; only let him come; he has no cause to fear my displeasure.

I know, I know that scandals must arise. It is no miracle that a man should fall, but it is a miracle that he should arise and stand. Peter fell, that he might know that he was a man; today the cedars of Lebanon, touching the sky with their tops, fall down. Wonder of wonders, even an angel fell from heaven and man in Paradise! What wonder is it, then, that a reed be shaken by the wind and a smoking flax be quenched? May the Lord Jesus teach you and use you and perfect you in every good work. Amen. Farewell.

—Brother Martin Luther, Professor of Theology, and Augustinian Vicar of the district of Meissen and Thuringe

As though his tasks were not enough, and responsibility that rested upon him insufficient to try his soul, the plague came to Wittenberg in the fall of 1516. Many citizens left immediately, and many of the monks were transferred temporarily to other cloisters. But Luther stayed in Wittenberg. Here his task was set, here his superiors had placed him, and here he would stay. Throughout his life this stalwart courage is discernible. Neither plague nor emperor nor pope were ever able to move him from his chosen course.

In 1516, the year before his public controversy, Luther was a well-recognized, self-controlled, intelligent leader in the affairs of his environment. The strong and steady discipline of the home in Mansfield stood him in good stead. The deep intensity of his religious struggles in Erfurt had been resolved into a quiet strength. His mind, his soul, and his physical strength were at work in the kingdom of the church.

By his position, he was obligated to recite the offices of the church at regular intervals daily, but the pressure of his many duties was so great day after day that he had little time for prayer or sleep. Unfriendly critics called this negligence. To Luther it was necessity. Many evenings he was too tired even to unclothe himself before falling asleep on his narrow cot in the cloister cell. He tried to catch up sometimes on his omitted prayers by reciting them all at once, when he found a break in his week's routine. He was truly in the "warfare of Christ," to which he had vowed himself when he had entered the Erfurt monastery.

On October 26, 1516, he wrote to John Lang, one of his closest friends:

Greeting:

I need a couple of amanuenses or secretaries, as I do almost nothing the livelong day but write letters. I do not know whether on that account I am always repeating myself, but you can judge. I am convent preacher, the reader at meals, am asked to deliver a sermon daily in the parish church, am district vicar (that is eleven times prior), business manager of our fish-farm at Litzkau, attorney in our case versus the Herzbergers now pending at Torgan, lecturer on St. Paul, assistant lecturer on the Psalter, besides having my correspondence, which, as I have said, occupies most of my time. I seldom have leisure to discharge the canonical services, to say nothing of attending to my own temptations with the world, the flesh, and the devil. You see how idle I am!

I think you must already have my answer about Brother John Metzel, but I will see what I can do. How in the world do you think I can get places for your epicures and sybarites? If you have brought them up in this pernicious way of life you ought to support them in the same pernicious style. I have enough useless brothers on all sides—if, indeed, any can be called useless to a patient soul. I have persuaded myself that the useless are the most useful of all—so you can have them a while longer. You write me that yesterday you began to lecture on the second book of the Sentences. I begin tomorrow to lecture on Galatians, though I fear the plague

*will not allow me to finish the course. The plague
takes off two or at most three in one day, and
that not every day. A son of the smith who lives
opposite was well yesterday and is buried today,
and another son lies ill. The epidemic began
rather severely and suddenly in the latter part of
the summer. You would persuade Bernhardi and
me to flee to you, but shall I flee? I hope the
world will not come to an end when Brother
Martin does. I shall send the brothers away if the
plague gets worse; I am stationed here and may
not flee because of my vow to obedience, until the
same authority which now commands me to stay
shall command me to go. Not that I do not fear
the plague (for I am not the Apostle Paul, but
only a lecturer on him), but I hope the Lord will
deliver me from my fear.*

The interests aroused inwardly by his personal experiences and teaching were all accentuated by his experience in the parish church. He found himself in a life strangely adapted to bring him information, almost as though fate were preparing him to be the focus for the problems of his age. In pastoral work, student direction, biblical study, philosophic speculation, private devotional life, and the many cares of administering eleven monasteries, Luther gathered experience that daily formed within him a broad, sensitive, accurate understanding of his environment.

A major disturbance to him was one of the sensitive spots in the old doctrine of "good works." This was the veneration of relics—the belief that the relics carried spiritual power. The elector of Saxony, Luther's own civil lord, had assembled hundreds of relics in the Wittenberg cathedral. Many of the claims for the relics were preposterous. Luther had seen several exhibits, in widely scattered places, of the "whole seamless robe of our Lord."

These and other absurdities disturbed the Wittenberg preacher greatly. Throughout 1515 and 1516 and into early 1517, a note of protest was sounded again and again in his sermons and lectures. Luther was in no sense a rebel. A devout son of the church, wholly in the atmosphere of the great historic piety of Catholicism, he labored in his chosen field. But he protested increasingly—not against thought or history, but against abuse.

Rome could not hold the lid on Europe's disaffection much longer. John Colet, Sir Thomas More, and others in England steadfastly had called for a higher, cleaner administration throughout the church. Erasmus had insisted that the church reform itself. Leaders of the church in Italy had banded into a society dedicated to reform. Throughout the length and breadth of western Christendom, the cry of scandal had been heard steadily for fifty years. The oncoming tide of reform was gathering resistless pressure. What it needed and longed for was accurate, consecrated, intelligent leadership.

The root cause was religious. Leadership thus had to come from religious sources. The Brethren of the Common Life, magnificent reformers in limited spheres, had not carried the attack far enough. Erasmus, with the whole school of the humanists, would not move into the field of pure religion. The churchmen in Italy were defeated because they lived too close to the source of the infection.

Here in far-off Wittenberg, so miserable and common that few people paid attention to it, was being formed a religious experience strong enough, intelligent enough, courageous enough to bring leadership. Yet Luther, so busy with his work, was unaware of anything except that he had discovered the source of the early piety of the church and that he could not be silent in the face of abuse. He was thoroughly conservative by nature. He loved his tradition, his church, and his people.

But he was honest. He hated sin in all places, high and low. He would protect his people. He would honor the obligations of his teaching office. He would speak clearly, decisively, directly.

Luther pleaded in lecture and sermon for the commoner, whose blood was his own. The strong claim of the people, rising steadily for half a century, now found a voice. He championed the peasant, challenging the right of the nobility to enact and enforce laws whereby they reserved game for themselves and punished severely—often with death—the poor for shooting one rabbit.

He called the great civil lords "robbers" or "sons of robbers." The oppression of the under classes by civil and ecclesiastical overlords moved him to fury, and he spoke openly against it. He severely condemned the greed and avarice that lies behind all war. He pronounced Julius II, Duke George of Saxony, Elector Frederick, and other princes guilty of this devastating petty warfare. He was a gloriously eloquent spokesman in the name of religion for all the mighty causes that uplift mankind. He "bore in his hands the banners of a nobler humanity." He fought without timidity. The elemental peasant blood was in him, and the lords and rulers must answer to the written word of Scripture for their unchristian exploitation of the sons of God.

Rome, with the abuses it created and lived upon, was the heretic! Martin Luther was the Catholic.

four

Lord of the Forest

The Freedom of a Christian Man
1517-1520

*H*ANS LUTHER WAS sitting one evening toward the middle of November 1517 by his home in Mansfield. One of his close friends and neighbors came over and handed him a long, closely printed, double-columned, single-sheet tract from Wittenberg. Hans read:

> Out of love for the truth and from a desire
> to elucidate it, the Reverend Father Martin
> Luther, Master of Arts in Sacred Theology,
> and ordinary lecturer therein at Wittenberg,
> intends to defend the following statements
> and dispute on them in that place.
> Therefore he asks that those who cannot be
> present to dispute with him orally shall do so
> in their absence by letter.
> In the name of our Lord Jesus Christ.
> Amen.

1. Our Lord and Master Jesus Christ in

saying, "Penitentiam agite," meant that the whole life of the faithful should be repentance.

2. And these words cannot refer to penance— that is confession and satisfaction.

. . . .

5. The Pope does not wish, nor is he able, to remit any penalty except what he or the Canon Law has imposed.

6. The Pope is not able to remit guilt except by declaring it forgiven by God—or in cases reserved to himself. . . .

. . . .

11. The erroneous opinion that canonical penance and punishment in purgatory are the same assuredly seems to be a tare sown while the bishops were asleep.

. . . .

28. It is certain that avarice is fostered by the money clinking in the chest, but to answer the prayers of the Church is in the power of God alone.

The paper shook in his hand, and great excitement possessed him as he realized with stunning force that his son was challenging the mightiest institution on earth. To Hans, Martin was still a boy, only 34. Yet those sentences spoke from the anvils of experience.

His eye returned to the page:

29. Who knows whether all the souls in
purgatory want to be freed?

. . . .

50. Christians are taught that if the Pope
knew exactions of the preachers of indulgences he would rather have St. Peter's
Church in ashes than have it built with the
flesh and bones of his sheep.

. . . .

62. The treasury of the Church is the power
of the keys given by Christ's merit.

. . . .

71. Who speaks against the apostolic truth of
indulgences, let him be anathema.

72. But who opposes the lust and license of
the preachers of pardons, let him be blessed.

. . . .

82. Why does not the Pope empty purgatory
from charity?

This sharp and incisive reasoning took Hans off guard.
Martin was right! If the pope could help those in
purgatory, then charity *should* move him to do so.

Hans closed his eyes a moment and felt intuitively the
approaching hour when Martin would be called to answer for this. The church would not brook such expo-
sure. But it *was* abusive of the church to do these things,
Hans thought, and he was thrilled that his flesh and blood
was so courageous.

92. Let all those prophets depart who say to

the people of Christ, peace, where there is no
peace.

93. But all those prophets do well who say to
the people of Christ, Cross, cross, and there is
no cross.

So Hans read slowly and thoughtfully the 95 propositions. He asked his neighbor what information the
messenger had brought from Wittenberg along with the
tract. He was told Martin had set this statement on the
bulletin board of the university at noon on All Saints Day.
The original had been in Martin's handwriting, and the
Wittenberg printers had rapidly published both Latin
and Greek texts for broadcast throughout Germany.

Hans thought over the past few years and remembered
how earnest Martin had been, how long and bitter had
been his soul's struggle for peace. He had thought, in
recent years, that Martin was speaking out rather boldly
against well-known practices of the church. He knew
that two years ago his son, in the Wittenberg pulpit, had
directly denounced the abuse of indulgences. He wondered if, after all the years of struggle and study, Martin
was about to step into an immense disaster.

The evening grew dark. Hans went inside and told
Margaret of Martin's challenge against indulgences. He
did not know the full background of the situation or
Martin's ultimate intention. But he knew that for a long
time he and his fellow citizens had balked under the
financial pressure and abuses of the church. If his boy,
now grown to manhood, could defend successfully a
more ancient and worthy practice, then the name of

Luther would be more highly distinguished than he had ever dreamed when he had envisioned Martin as a lawyer.

Mansfield and the rest of Germany and Europe throughout November and December excitedly discussed the issues raised by the theses on indulgences. In Wittenberg, Martin Luther was sure the whole indulgence practice had come to such abuse that a direct attack was the only hope for it. He had been brought to this public contest by long and careful preparation. In his search for an honest piety, he had come to discount heavily the penitential customs of the church.

In the Wittenberg parish in 1517, his people had come to him with letters of indulgence they had bought. On the basis of these letters, they argued for release from certain consequences of sinning. He could hold his peace no longer.

Unwilling to believe the stories told to him by his parishioners, he procured the letter of instructions given by Albert, Archbishop of Magdeburg, to the commissioner who had sold the indulgences. In these instructions he found confirmation for all the positions maintained by the Wittenberg people.

He knew Archbishop Albert—a prince in the house of Brandenburg, Archbishop of Magdeburg and acting Bishop of Halberstadt, had secured likewise his election to the archbishopric of Mayence. But he did not know that in order to secure himself in these three bishoprics—which canon law forbade him to hold—Albert had made a financial bargain with the papacy. Luther did not know the House of Fugger, Augsburg bankers, had loaned Albert the money for the bribe and fees he had paid to

Leo X for confirmation. Nor did he know representatives of Albert and Leo had met and discussed the price to be paid. Leo's representatives had said 12,000 ducats, for the 12 apostles. Albert's representatives had said 7 ducats, for the 7 deadly sins. They had compromised on 10,000 ducats.

Luther did not know that in order to make sure the financial transaction would be carried through, Leo had granted Albert the privilege of selling an indulgence. He did not know half the proceeds of this sale would go to Albert, from which he would pay his debts to the bankers; the other half would go to Leo. He did not know the whole proceeds of the sale of the indulgence was supposed to go to the rebuilding of St. Peter's Church.

The inner workings of this—one of the most scandalous operations in the history of the church—were unknown to Luther. All he knew was that the clear and expressed intention of Christian piety had been brutally and inexcusably broken by this particular indulgence sale.

He sat in his study in the Black Cloister and argued with himself through August, September, and October, while the sale went on. Luther's own prince, the elector of Saxony, was too wise to allow his subjects to be bled for Rome and refused permission for the selling of the indulgences in his territory. He knew well the old proverb, "When Rome comes by, draw your purse strings tight."

Thus Wittenberg did not see the indulgence seller. But Luther's people walked just a few miles to the west and bought their indulgence tickets at the town of Zerbst, or a few miles to the east at Juterbog. Both of these towns, outside the dominion of the elector, were visited by the commissioner for the indulgence.

Luther could not believe what his people told him was true. He knew the church believed Christ had stored up great benefits for the human race by means of His passion. He knew the church believed the heroic Christian activity of the saints benefited the common Christian. He knew the church believed the Bishop of Rome held the "power of the Keys." He believed these things, too. But this sale was different.

The prior of the Dominican convent at Leipzig, John Tetzel, was selling these indulgences. When he entered Juterbog where Luther's people went to see and hear him, he had the papal bull, announcing the indulgence, carried on velvet cloth at the head of a procession. With great pomp and ceremony he marched through the streets of the town to the place of preaching. There, in unbelievable boldness, he promised to the Saxons that they could buy release from all punishment imposed by church law; they also could buy release from the penances they must do in purgatory for their sins.

With mock pathos and brutal hypocrisy, he painted for the benefit of his hearers the sufferings of their dead relatives in purgatory and told them point-blank that they could release their loved ones from suffering by paying a little money. Duped by these promises, the unlettered Germans whom Luther looked upon as his sheep believed the great reward of character thus could be bought.

The Black Cloister became the scene of a furious battle in Luther's heart and mind. How could the heads of the church act like this? Did they not understand the limits of papal power? Did they not know the mercy of Christ is not for sale—or was everything for sale in Rome? He had heard that everything was.

Furious at the way the sacred things of life thus were destroyed, but cool and determined in mind, he quietly wrote out 95 distinct sentences, each of which was a debatable point in the whole question of the office of penance—particularly the indulgence phase. These things, he thought, should be cleared up. And he, as a teacher of theology and possessor of the sacred right of clarifying Scripture, was in a position to express himself.

So on October 31, 1517, when Wittenberg was crowded for the anniversary of the consecration of the Cathedral Church, he posted his 95 sentences with a brief pre-amble. The wooden doors of the Cathedral Church were used as the bulletin board, since the church was attached to the school. It was not as though Luther took a hammer, symbolic of revolution, and struck at the portals of this church, symbolic of the whole church. Rather, here was a theology professor and village preacher calling his colleagues to dispute, in correct academic fashion, the fundamental questions of the generation.

He did not even print his statement, as two months before he had printed and sent to most of his friends a similar list of theses on the weaknesses of scholastic theology. He had been disappointed that these had not stirred up more discussion.

He was totally unprepared, however, for the torrential way these theses on indulgences swept through Europe. They appeared in every language and every place in Christendom "as though carried by angelic messengers."

The great painter Albrecht Dürer was drawn to Luther's vigorous leadership and would remain his admirer throughout the struggle of the Reformation. On this occasion, he sent to Luther through a mutual friend a series of his woodcuts.

The strong, sturdy, quiet teacher in Wittenberg now found himself the rallying leader for the disaffection of half a century. Hans Luther's son was forced to direct a campaign for the clarification of the Gospel and the reform of the church.

Luther had no intention of conducting any of this work under cover. With the publication of his theses he wrote a letter to Albert, who had to bear the responsibility for the indulgence sale. The letter was dated the same day the theses were posted.

> *Grace and the mercy of God and whatever else may be and is!*
>
> *Forgive me, Very Reverend Father in Christ, and illustrious Lord, that I, the offscouring of men, have the temerity to think of a letter to your high mightiness. . . .*
>
> *Papal indulgences for the building of St. Peter's are hawked about under your illustrious sanction. I do not now accuse the sermons of the preachers who advertise them, for I have not seen the same, but I regret that the people have conceived about them the most erroneous ideas. Forsooth these unhappy souls believe that if they buy letters of pardon they are sure of their salvation; likewise that souls fly out of purgatory as soon as money is cast into the chest; in short, that the grace conferred is so great that there is no sin whatever which cannot be absolved thereby, even*

*if, as they say, taking an impossible example, a
man should violate the mother of God. They also
believe that indulgences free them from all penalty and guilt.*

*My God! thus are the souls committed, Father,
to your charge, instructed unto death, for which
you have a fearful and growing reckoning to pay.
. . .*

*What else could I do, excellent Bishop and
illustrious Prince, except pray your Reverence for
the sake of the Lord Jesus Christ to take away
your Instructions to the Commissioners altogether
and impose some other form of preaching on the
proclaimers of pardons, lest perchance someone
should at length arise and confute them and their
Instructions publicly, to the great blame of your
Highness. This I vehemently deprecate, yet I fear
it may happen unless the grievance is quickly
redressed. . . .*

*Your unworthy son,
Martin Luther, Augustinian, Dr. Theol.*

Initiation of a movement opposing Luther came from
Albert on receipt of this letter. He brought the matter to
the attention of Rome, for the work of Luther had been
so successful in diminishing the confidence of the people
in the indulgences that the sales had been seriously
curtailed. But the head of the church in Rome was in no
mood to give serious consideration to a question of piety.
The son of Lorenzo the Magnificent, tonsured at 7,
made a cardinal at 14, given voting power in the Curia at

17, Giovanni d'Medici was elected to the papacy in February 1513. He was ordained a priest the next month, made a bishop two days later, and installed in the papal office two days after that, taking the name Leo X. He is reported to have said to his brother when informed of his election, "Let us now enjoy the papacy, since God has given it to us." Regardless of whether the quotation is accurate, its central idea of enjoyment is a true description of Leo's intention.

Cultured, refined, agreeable, and exceptionally clever, Leo was well-equipped to bring the papacy to new Renaissance heights. The art of Italy was in his debt. In financial affairs, he was a tremendous spender and not a successful gainer, so his papacy was always troubled. Supposedly a kind man, he nevertheless ruthlessly executed several cardinals suspected of poisoning. Completely immersed in secular affairs, he could not understand the religious issue of this northern quarrel. He was surrounded by counselors utterly incapable of statesmanlike action on the issues raised by Luther.

The brilliant heir of the Medicean Renaissance, enthroned in Rome, surrounded by the finest art and poetry in Europe, was matched with the son of Thuringian peasants. In this battle, Leo X—many times the victor in matters of literature, politics, art, and the refinements of living—was unequipped to meet a man whose sole interest was practical religion.

Luther wrote to the pope in May 1518. He told him he had always accepted papal authority and in no way desired to appear heretical, but the recent papal indulgence had spread grave scandal and mockery, driving him to protest the abuse. Luther now desired only that the pope should understand his position and carefully consider the matters at issue.

Careful consideration was not something Leo X was prepared to give. He allowed the situation to develop rather haphazardly.

The attempt to control Luther began—as it should have begun—through his order. Leo thought the theses had been composed by a drunken monk who would see things clearer when he was sober. He instructed the general of the Augustinian Order to quench these fires of rebellion. Accordingly, the matter was brought up at the meeting of the order at Heidelberg in May 1518.

Luther was present, as was his friend Staupitz. The brothers discussed quietly the position of the accused; Luther explained and defended his theses. Some brothers agreed with him; some disagreed. Luther thought the issue was serious, and he did not want to involve his order, so he resigned as district vicar. His successor was one of his closest friends.

Luther's mind obviously was unchanged after the Heidelberg meeting. One young, enthusiastic conservative at the meeting told Luther he dared not teach such doctrines to the peasants, or they would stone him to death. But Luther had read the temper of the peasants more correctly. He was not in danger of his life, and he returned to Wittenberg to await the next move—but Tetzel, who had sold the indulgences, was afraid to move outside his cloister at Leipzig.

At one o'clock in the afternoon of August 25, 1518, 22-year-old Philip Melanchthon entered Wittenberg. He had come to teach Greek. The establishment of chairs of Greek had been slow in the northern universities, and he was the first teacher of Greek to be invited to Wittenberg.

Luther had urged the appointment of another candidate and looked on Melanchthon with considerable anxiety. His anxiety vanished four days later when Melanchthon delivered his installation address to the university faculty. Melanchthon made impassioned pleas for an orientation of the curriculum around the humanities and the New Testament.

At 35, Luther was at his greatest strength; Melanchthon was at the very beginning of his career. A steadfast friendship sprang up between them instantly, never to be broken until death. The ability and devotion of Melanchthon became more important each day to Luther. Now he had at his elbow the finest humanist Germany had yet produced. Melanchthon was a nephew of John Reuchlin, a pioneer of Hebrew studies in Europe and a great admirer of Erasmus—chief of the European humanists. He came to Wittenberg thoroughly enthusiastic over the humanistic movement in its Christian sphere. As he argued before the faculty and students at Wittenberg for a union of classical and Pauline studies, Luther's heart rejoiced. The fine, sensitive, accurate, grammatical scholarship of Melanchthon was joined to the powerful, emotional dynamic of Luther.

When Melanchthon published a commentary on the letter to the Colossians, Luther wrote in the preface:

> I am rough, boisterous, stormy, and alto-
> gether warlike.
> I am born to fight against innumerable
> monsters and devils. I must remove stumps
> and stones, cut away thistles and thorns, and

clear the wild forests; but Master Philip
comes along, softly and gently, sowing and
watering, with joy, according to the gifts
which God has abundantly bestowed upon
him.

For the remainder of their lives, including the fiercest
days of public battle, Luther and Melanchthon were
accustomed to meet in the little garden behind
Melanchthon's home, at a stony table. Their little boys
would play together in childhood.

Rome, meanwhile, did not let the case rest. Luther was
forced to defend his action before a representative of the
pope in Augsburg. Initially, in August 1518, he had been
ordered to appear in person in Rome, but the Augsburg
meeting was substituted. Luther was glad for the change,
for he knew—as every leader of his age knew—that to
step within the control of his enemies now was to meet
death.

He journeyed to Augsburg in October and met Cardinal
Cajetan, the general of the Dominican Order. The
cardinal, true to the Dominican type, was zealous for
papal rights. His master, Leo X, in 1516 had reinforced
the belief in the supreme authority of the papacy over a
church council. Cardinal Cajetan was unwilling even to
let Luther talk.

Luther, on the other hand, had come to Augsburg
expecting to defend himself. At the first meeting, he fell
on his face before the cardinal and accorded him the
respect of his rank. But they could get nowhere. Luther
tried to interrupt the cardinal's steady flow of contradiction and abuse, and the cardinal shouted louder and

louder until Luther himself finally lost his moderation and shouted likewise.

The conference ended in thorough misunderstanding. The cardinal insisted that Luther recant. Luther insisted on discussing the issue. The cardinal claimed heresy. Luther challenged him to prove any statement of the theses to be heretical; the cardinal was unable to do so.

Friends tried to effect a reconciliation. Luther apologized for his conduct at their second meeting, and the cardinal accepted the apology. But at the third and last meeting it was the same story: a call for recantation and a refusal.

Luther withdrew from the audience and waited a few days in Augsburg. He heard rumors that a trap was laid for his arrest. So by night, he quietly left the city, riding steadily to the north. Both horse and rider were thin and haggard.

On his return, he wrote a description of his meeting with Cardinal Cajetan for public reading. He also wrote a letter to Pope Leo, which he called "An appeal from the Pope ill informed to the Pope well informed."

The next attempt at reconciliation was conducted by Charles von Miltitz, a papal ambassador to the Elector Frederick. This attempt was colored by political necessities. The Diet* of the Holy Roman Empire was soon to meet for the election of an emperor, and the pope wanted the favor of Elector Frederick so he could control Frederick's vote in the election. The elector was a devout Catholic, never in sympathy with Luther's theology, but he was a staunch defender of the rights of his subjects. He refused to be a party to an intrigue that would

---

* Formal assembly of princes

surrender Luther without a fair defense.

Miltitz failed in his attempt to conciliate the parties. But in January 1519, he won from Luther a promise to write the pope a letter of apology for the whole business. Luther promised to agree to support indulgences in their proper sense and urge steady reverence for the Holy See. But the mission of Miltitz was disowned by his superiors and came to naught.

The next stage in the controversy was far more dramatic than any before. John Eck was a professor of theology at the University of Ingolstadt, a Dominican monk, and a man of considerable ability in debating. He challenged Luther and his Wittenberg colleague, Andrew Bodenstein, to a public discussion in Leipzig.

The issues were not at all clear. Luther could not be classed with the heretics. Bodenstein was more impetuous and apt to go off half-cocked. If Eck could succeed in wringing from either of them heretical statements, then Rome could silence both men.

Eck was masterful at this. Leipzig was in the unfriendly territory of Duke George of Saxony. The University of Leipzig was jealous of the growing prestige of the University of Wittenberg. Tetzel's home convent was in Leipzig. Everything looked bad for Luther.

He was considerably disturbed as he set forth from Wittenberg. But the faculty and students of his home university would not let him go alone. The professors rode in two country carts, while 200 students, thoroughly armed, walked beside and behind them. With Luther rode Melanchthon, Justus Jonas, Nicholas Amsdorf, Andrew Bodenstein, and Duke Barnim, the rector of the university.

When the Wittenberg group arrived in Leipzig there was a constant menace of rioting. They kept guards placed in the inns where they lodged. They went in groups, well-armed, from inn to church and to the council chamber where the debate was to be held. Leipzig itself furnished extra police to keep order.

After a preliminary debate between Eck and Bodenstein, Luther entered the lists July 4, 1519. They were assembled in the largest hall of Duke George's own palace, and the duke was present. Eck was the dominant figure. According to one account:

> He had a huge square body, a full strong
> voice coming from his chest; fit for a tragic
> actor or a town crier, more harsh than dis-
> tinct; his mouth, eyes and whole aspect gave
> one the idea of a butcher or a soldier rather
> than of a theologian. He gave one the idea of
> a man striving to overcome his opponent
> rather than of one striving to win a victory for
> the truth. There was as much sophistry as
> good reasoning in his arguments; he was
> continually misquoting his opponent's words
> or trying to give them a meaning they were
> not intended to convey.

When Luther rose to speak, he appeared to the same eyewitness as:

> . . . of medium height; his body is slender,
> emaciated by study and by cares; one can
> count almost all the bones; he stands in the

> prime of his age; his voice sounds clear and
> distinct—however hard his opponent pressed
> him he maintained his calmness and his good
> nature, though in debate he sometimes used
> bitter words. . . . He carried a bunch of flow-
> ers in his hand, and when the discussion
> became hot he looked at it and smelled it.

Maintained good nature . . . used bitter words in debate . . . carried flowers!

The debate moved into a field where Luther did not want it. Eck constantly shifted from the present considerations to past records. He wanted to drive Luther into admitting a position similar to that held by heretical groups throughout church history. If that could be done, then he could set the label of "heretic" on the Wittenberger.

Eck tried the Waldensian history, but to no avail. Then he called forth the activity of Wycliffe, but Luther was not caught. Finally he brought up the work of John Hus. After a particularly vigorous expression of opinion by Eck, Luther interrupted him. "But good Dr. Eck, every Hussite opinion is not wrong."

At this Duke George, who looked distrustfully upon everything Hussite, whispered, "That's the plague."

Eck was jubilant. He countered Luther with the challenge that the church had denounced the Hussite opinions, that the Council of Constance had condemned them, that the pope had declared them heretical. Luther was driven finally with remorseless logic to the damning admission that popes and councils could err.

The Leipzig debates ended. Eck started southward to Rome, triumphant. He had unmasked another heretic.

Tetzel was overjoyed, hiding from the wrath of the people he had duped. The Wittenberger and his friends journeyed homeward. Luther left Leipzig branded a "heretic, rebel, a thing to flout."

Luther sensed deeply that dark days were ahead of him. But he felt strength, too. The days of indecision were over. Now he was out in the open. He could move quite clearly now.

The winter of 1519-20 passed uneventfully in Wittenberg while the opposing forces gathered their strength. Luther, Melanchthon, and their colleagues talked steadily, corresponded at length with friends all over Europe, and prepared themselves for the next meeting.

It came in the early summer of 1520. On June 15, Leo signed the bull *Exurge Domine*. This was the work of Eck, not of Leo himself. It called upon Luther to recant within 60 days or be excommunicated. It affirmed the heretical quality of Luther's position in opposing the sale of indulgences, and it did so in open defiance of the finest thought of the historic Catholic Church. Framed by Leo's belligerent advisers, headed by Eck, it caused further disaffection rather than healing of the church. In many of the northern provinces, people now were so thoroughly on Luther's side that they refused to allow the bull to be published. It often was torn into bits and scattered in the streets.

When it came to Wittenberg, it met a royal reception. After long consideration, Martin Luther had decided to handle it directly, as though it were, in reality, open warfare.

Early on the morning of December 10, the students in Wittenberg read this notice on their bulletin board:

> Let whosoever adheres to the truth of the
> Gospel be present at nine o'clock at the
> Church of the Holy Cross outside the walls,
> where the impious books of papal decrees and
> scholastic theology will be burnt according to
> ancient and apostolic usage, inasmuch as the
> boldness of the enemies of the Gospel has
> waxed so great that they daily burn the
> evangelic books of Luther. Come, pious and
> zealous youth, to this pious and religious
> spectacle, for perchance now is the time
> when the Antichrist must be revealed!

A few hours later Luther headed a march of the students and faculty out through a gate in the city wall to a nearby field. There a huge bonfire was prepared and one of the university professors set the fire. Then, with quiet dignity, Martin Luther himself placed the books of the canon law on the fire, in token of his refusal to be bound by them. Then, taking the bull directed against him and calling for his recantation, he placed it on the fire with the words:

> Because thou hast brought down the truth
> of God, He also brings thee down to this fire
> today. Amen.

Luther and the faculty returned to the university halls, while the students stayed long in mock parade, singing around the bonfire. They finally left solemnly, singing the "Te Deum."

In the summer of 1520, Luther presented his reasoned

opinions on the entire question to the Christian public. In three famous pamphlets he drew up his offensive and defensive positions. In August he published *To the Christian Nobility of the German Nation on the Improvement of the Christian Estate*. Here, with clear, forceful logic and powerful emotion, he attacked the sole, arbitrary authority of the papacy. In the spirit of growing nationalism, he appealed to the German people to free themselves from the tyranny of papal power. He contradicted the famous Roman positions that the clergy are superior to the laity in controlling the church, that only the pope may interpret Scripture authoritatively, and that only the pope may call a church council. These, he said, were the three walls behind which the power of Rome had hidden itself. All of them, he maintained, are invalid in light of the great essential doctrine of the priesthood of all believers. There is no essential distinction between priest and people. Each Christian is, in spiritual reality, a priest.

To German ears, this was a glorious appeal for freedom from Italian control. Even his bitter antagonist, Duke George, admitted a thrill of exaltation as he read this call to Germany. On one hand, a nationalistic view prompted its writing. But on the other hand was a deeper, more powerful sense of the immortal doctrine of the priesthood of all believers.

Hardly had Europe caught its breath from this powerful attack on what was considered a centuries-old authority when Luther published in October a work intended to undermine still further the power of the Roman church. *On the Babylonian Captivity of the Church* examined the sacramental system of the Roman church, a system built up during the same few centuries preceding

Luther which had seen the rise of the pope's autocratic power. Luther maintained no sacrament was valid if it could not find justification in the New Testament.

Starting from the New Testament premise, Luther could justify wholly only the Eucharist and baptism. There was partial justification also, he admitted, for the sacrament of penance. Christians were in captivity like the Jews of old in Babylon; the seven sacraments of Rome were the chains by which the captor, Rome, held them in slavery. There was no sacramental quality, in the true sense, to confirmation, marriage, holy orders ,or extreme unction. These might be great Christian customs worthy of the church's blessing, but they were not sacraments.

The Roman church held everyone in fear by means of the sacrament. The true Christian church, Luther believed, should be built only upon the three valid sacraments.

In November 1520, Luther followed these aggressive documents with the sensitive, lovely presentation of the center of his own belief, *The Freedom of the Christian Man*. Here he stated the paradox:

> A Christian man is the most free lord of all,
> subject to no one.
> A Christian man is the dutiful servant of all,
> subject to everyone.

From this he wrung a glorious presentation of the free spiritual life of the Christian believer. The grace of God, accepted by faith, makes the Christian lord of the universe. He may starve in a dungeon or reign from a prince's throne, and still possess inwardly the glorious freedom of the children of God. It is a free gift, made possible by faith in Christ. But because he is thus free, the Christian is bound by the great law of Christian love and by the indwelling spirit of Christ to serve in perfect charity all mankind.

So the freedom that belongs to a Christian is the freedom created by the indwelling spirit of Christ, and it leads to constant Christian service. It is Paul's old and well-loved doctrine of the "fruits of the spirit."

Remembering his pledge to Miltitz, he sent this document to Leo X. He wrote a letter to accompany the little tract, which read in part:

Of your person, excellent Leo, I have heard only what is honorable and good . . . but of the Roman See, as you and all men must know, it is more scandalous and shameful than any Sodom or Babylon, and, as far as I can see, its wickedness is beyond all counsel and help, having become desperate and abysmal. It made me sick at heart to see that under your name and that of the Roman Church, the poor people in all the world are cheated and injured, against which thing I have set myself and will set myself as long as I have life, not that I hope to reform that horrible Roman Sodom, but that I know I am the debtor and servant of all Christians, and that it is my duty to counsel and warn them . . . .

Finally, that I come not before your Holiness without a gift, I offer you this little treatise, dedicated to you as an augury of peace and good hope; by this book you may see how fruitfully I

*might employ my time, as I should prefer to, if
only those impious flatterers of yours would let
me. It is a little book as respects size, but if I
mistake not, the whole sum of a Christian life is
set down therein, in respect to contents. I am
poor and have nothing else to send you, nor do
you stand in need of any but my spiritual gifts.*

This letter and pamphlet had been sent to Rome two
months before the bonfire in Wittenberg that signaled
the open rebellion.

THE EPIC HOUR
1521

Through the winter of 1520-21, Luther was active in all
his regular work. He preached daily—often twice a day.
He taught his regular classes in the university. He wrote
commentaries on Genesis and the Psalms. He published
a sensitive, tender commentary on the Magnificat, "in
which Mary's canticle became again the song of the
lowly and the meek." He answered the criticism of his
enemies with insults and biting sarcasm of his own. The
division was becoming more severe daily, and men were
being called on for decisions.

It saddened Luther tremendously to find his beloved
Staupitz unwilling to take to the open rebellion. Staupitz
was well along in years now and had retired to Salzburg.
He had written to Luther in September 1518:

Possess your soul in patience for salvation. I have enough to write to fill a book, but will express myself briefly. It seems to me that the world is exasperated against Truth; with so great a hatred was Christ once crucified, and today I see nothing waiting for you but the Cross. Unless I mistake, the opinion prevails that no one should examine Scripture without leave of the Pope in order to find for himself, which Christ certainly commands us to do. You have a few defenders, and would that they were not hiding for fear of enemies. I should like you to leave Wittenberg and come to me, that we may live and die together. This would also please the archbishop. Here I finish. It is expedient thus to be, that abandoned we may follow abandoned Christ. Farewell, and a good journey to you.

Luther wrote to him in October 1519, after Leipzig:

. . . Now about myself. What will you? You are leaving me. I have been sad for you today as a weaned child for his mother. I pray you praise the Lord even in a sinner like me. I hate my wretched life; I fear death; I am empty of faith and full of qualities which, Christ knows, I should much prefer to do without, were it not to serve Him thereby. . . . Last night I dreamed about you. I dreamed that you were leaving me while I wept bitterly, but you waved to me and told me to cease weeping, for you would come

back to me, which indeed, has happened this very day. But now, farewell, and pray for me in my wretchedness.

Staupitz wrote in January 1521 to their mutual friend Link: "Martin has undertaken a hard task and acts with great courage illuminated by God; I stammer and am a child needing milk."

Finally the old vicar wrote an open letter in which he tried to be conciliatory, but which bore evidence of his allegiance to Rome. This was not an hour for hesitation, and Luther gently wrote him:

Greeting. I wonder, reverend Father, that my letters and pamphlets have not reached you, as I gather from your letter to Link that they have not. Intercourse with men takes so much of my time that preaching unto others I have myself become a castaway.

At Worms they have as yet done nothing against me, although the papists contrive harm with extraordinary fury. Yet Spalatin writes the Evangelic cause has so much favor there that he does not expect I shall be condemned unheard. . . .

I have heard with no great pain that you are attacked by Pope Leo, for thus the cross you have preached to others you may exemplify yourself. I hope that wolf, for you honor him too much to call him a Lion [Leo], will not be satisfied with your declaration, which will be interpreted to mean that you deny me and mine, inasmuch as you submit to the Pope's judgment.

If Christ love you he will make you revoke that declaration, since the Pope's bull must condemn all you have hitherto taught and believed about the mercy of God. As you knew this would be the case, it seems to me that you offend Christ in proposing Leo for a judge, whom you see to be an enemy of Christ running wild [debacchari] against the Word of his grace. You should have stood up for Christ and have contradicted the Pope's impiety. This is not the time to tremble but to cry aloud, while our Lord Jesus Christ is being condemned, burned, and blasphemed. Wherefore as much as you exhort me to humility, I exhort you to pride. You are too yielding. I am too stiff-necked.

Indeed it is a solemn matter. We see Christ suffer. Should we keep silence and humble ourselves? Now that our dearest Saviour, who gave Himself for us, is made a mock in the world, should we not fight and offer our lives for Him? Dear father, the present crisis is graver than many think. Now applies the great gospel text, "Whosoever shall confess me before men, him shall the Son of man also confess before the angels of God, for whosoever shall be ashamed of me and of my words, of him shall the Son of man be ashamed, when he shall come in his own glory." May I be found guilty of pride, avarice, adultery, murder, opposition to the Pope, and all other sins, rather than be silent when the Lord suffers and says, "I looked on my right hand, and beheld, but there was no man that would know

me; refuge failed me: no man cared for my soul."
By confessing Him I hope to be absolved from all
my sins. Wherefore I have raised my horns with
confidence against the Roman idol, and the true
Antichrist. The word of Christ is not the word of
peace, but the word of the sword. But why should
I, a fool, teach a wise man?

Luther stopped a moment in his writing here, and thought of the days when Staupitz was his great comfort. How wise and gentle the man had been with him. Why could he not see the vital conflict between that blessed piety he had taught and the terrible abuse of the present system? Not knowing how all-important the issue was, Staupitz was about to halt between two opinions.

The pen touched paper again, and Luther poured out his plea to hold his once matchless teacher.

I write this more confidently because I fear you
will take a middle course between Christ and the
Pope, who are now, as you see, in bitter strife.
But let us pray that the Lord Jesus with the
breath of His mouth will destroy this son of
perdition. If you do not wish to, at least let me go
and be bound. With Christ's aid I will not keep
still about this monster's crimes before his face.

Truly your submission has saddened me not a
little, and has shown me that you are different
from that Staupitz who was the herald of grace
and of the cross. If you had said what you did
before you knew of the bull and of the shame of
Christ, you would not have saddened me.

> *Hutton and many others write strongly for me,*
> *and daily those songs are sung which delight not*
> *Babylon. Our elector acts as constantly, as pru-*
> *dently and faithfully, and at his command I am*
> *publishing my Defense in both languages. . . .*

Intimation that he would be called to the Imperial Diet came to Luther throughout the winter. Charles V, newly elected head of the Holy Roman Empire, was holding his first diet at Worms, a German town on the Rhine. It opened January 25, 1521, to consider all the affairs of the empire.

One of the minor questions, technically, was "To take notice of the books and descriptions made by Friar Martin Luther against the Court of Rome." Before the arrival of the imperial party at Worms, the question of how to handle the Luther issue had been discussed. Frederick the Elector had met Charles and his retinue at Cologne in October and November 1520. Frederick carried a letter from Luther to the emperor asking for protection and a fair trial. The two men talked over the possibilities, and the emperor promised Frederick that Luther would be treated lawfully.

Then Frederick had a conference with the papal representatives to the court of Charles, who demanded that all Luther's work be burned and that Luther be delivered up bound. Frederick sent for Erasmus, then in Cologne, and asked, "Has Luther erred?"

"Yes, he has erred in two points: in attacking the crown of the pope and the bellies of the monks," answered the greatest of the humanists.

"What is to be done?" asked Frederick.

Erasmus drew up twenty-two axioms, proving that the pope should appoint an impartial tribunal for the consideration of Luther's propositions. So Frederick decided to stand by Luther and see him through at the coming diet.

The bull "Exurge Domine" only had threatened excommunication. But Luther's reception of it had brought an end to the matter, and on January 3, 1521, Leo X signed the final bull demanding complete excommunication. So when the Roman party acted at Worms, they acted on the principle that Luther was already condemned. He should not be heard. He should be executed as a heretic. The civil authority was not bound to keep faith with a heretic. He should either recant or die; even if he recanted, it was not certain he should live.

The representatives of Rome were Jerome Aleander and Marino Caracciola. Alexander was the chief. He was librarian of the Vatican, was later to be a cardinal, knew Greek and the classics, and had lectured at Paris. By temperament he was an inquisitor. It was easy for him to light bonfires for books or men. He could see men die for the glory of God without a troubled conscience. He had killed five peasants because of the loss of a favorite dog. (And Luther was blamed for a peasants' revolt!) At Worms, he held to one line of reasoning: Luther must die!

On February 13, Aleander spoke to the diet for three hours, demanding that Luther be condemned without a hearing. But to Luther the quarrel was not concluded. The question was open. He was a spokesman for a living, growing movement.

On March 26, Luther, working in Wittenberg, received the summons from Charles V. It addressed him as "honored, dear, and pious son" and called on him to appear in order "to obtain information about certain doctrines originating with you and certain books written by you."

Luther was no coward, but he knew the game he played now. The sensitive balance could break at any moment, and he would be in the hands of the enemy. But he would not stay away. He had been born for this hour. Now the emperor, the papal representative, and the German people would hear his blessed doctrine. His life was not the issue.

On April 2, he left for Worms. Melanchthon wanted to go, but Luther would not have it, saying, "Dear brother, if I do not come back, if my enemies put me to death, you go on teaching and standing fast in the truth. If you live, my death will matter little."

Crowds waved them off. The magistrates of the city hired a driver and horses for the open country wagon, half-filled with straw, in which they rode. Amsdorf, Peter Swaven—a Danish student who also had gone armed to Leipzig in 1519, and John Petzensteiner, Peter's Augustinian companion, were with Luther. Caspar Sturm, the imperial herald, rode ahead on horseback, carrying the royal coat-of-arms, a square, yellow banner with a black, two-headed eagle. Luther carried his lute, to while away the long hours in the inns.

Over the old familiar road they traveled to Leipzig, where townspeople, magistrates, and students gave them a cordial welcome. From Leipzig they proceeded to Weimar, where his now enthusiastic friend Justus Jonas joined him. As they rode on to Erfurt, Luther wondered how he would be received in the place where his happy student days had led him steadily toward the high calling of God. Erfurt was where his vows had been taken. He remembered the vow—"the warfare of Christ"—and knew indeed its deep fulfilment.

He was anxious as they neared the city. Great joy welled up in his heart as he saw a long procession of students and faculty headed by the rector come to meet him. The magistrates gave a banquet in his honor. Erfurt's distinguished son had returned in fame.

He slept in his old Augustinian monastery. Sunday morning, April 7, he preached in the cathedral where his youthful heart once had been stirred. The crowded church balcony creaked under its weight, and people began to rush for the door, but Luther stopped them. "Be still, dear people. It is only a joke of the devil. Be still. There is no danger."

From Erfurt they journeyed over well-known paths to Eisenach. Everywhere he was received with great applause. Exhausted, he was ill at Eisenach. Physicians bled him, but God cured him, he said, after a good stiff cordial and a long sleep.

Leaving Eisenach, he drew nearer the danger zone. He stopped to visit schools and preach in Frankfurt, not far from Worms. Again and again, friends interceded to stop his approach. Sturm, the herald, pointed out the emperor's March edict to seize all Luther's books, and asked if he should proceed to Worms. Luther's reply was yes.

Efforts were made to get him to stop at Ebernburg, a day's journey from Worms. Ebernburg was a fine castle owned by Francis von Sickingen, who was able and willing to give Luther protection. But he would not be stopped. The pressure of destiny was in him.

At Offenheim, he sent a terse, courageous reply to

Spalatin, the elector's secretary who had repeatedly warned him of the impending dangers: "I shall go to Worms though there were as many devils there as tiles on the roofs." So the little procession moved onward.

Just before ten in the morning of Tuesday, April 16, the cathedral tower watchman blew his horn loudly to announce the party's arrival. Thousands gathered along the road, and Luther rode in his humble wagon triumphantly into Worms. The papal legate wrote to Rome that Luther stepped from the vehicle saying, "God will be with me," and looking around at the people with "demoniacal" eyes.

He was put up at the house of the Knights of St. John. There the crowd gathered rapidly and kept him busy with visitors until late into the night. Aleander said all the world went to see Luther. Friends and supporters were at the inn, and at "the Swan" nearby.

Wednesday morning he prepared for his appearance, finding time to administer the last sacrament to a dying Saxon noble who sent for him. At four in the afternoon the day after his arrival, the herald and the imperial marshal came to the inn for him.

Luther was dressed in his black Augustinian gown. He was sturdy, large-boned, but not stout. His eyes were set deep and glowed with exceptional brightness. Tonsure newly shaved, he was crowned with a circle of thick, black hair. Cranach's painting of him that year shows clearly the strong, resolute, fiery, and animated features. He was in his thirty-eighth year, his heart still unsoiled by the terrors of public warfare, his mind still vigorous, his spirit undampened by the long stresses of defeat and compromise. Peasant strength, monastic training, personal piety, elemental honesty, and courage were all his.

The crowds were so thick in the main streets that the men went through gardens from house to house to the hallway entrance in the bishop's palace. Luther stood outside about two hours. Finally, at six o'clock, he was ushered into the meeting of the diet.

It was dark outside. Great, smoking lamps lit the hot, stuffy room, overcrowded with dignitaries. On the way in he saw an old friend and spoke to him.

Charles V was the central figure. Only twenty years old, pale, quiet, he was surrounded by all his counselors. Six electors of the empire were there, including the Elector Frederick, Luther's own civil lord. The papal legates were there, unable to control events completely. Bishops, princes, deputies, and ambassadors filled the hall. Spanish and German soldiers were on guard. Thousands of persons jammed the passageways and doors.

Before Charles V in person and Leo X in representation, the son of Hans Luther stood quietly for a moment. Looking around, he saw Aleander glaring at him. "So the Jews must have looked at Christ," he thought.

His gaze finally came to rest on the youthful emperor. Their eyes met, but not their spirits. Each failed to read the strength in the other. Luther saw Charles surrounded by his court, and he seemed to Luther like "some poor lamb amid swine and hounds."

His reverie was broken by a movement before him. He watched an official rise and turn to him. He was told that his case was now before the diet and he was to say nothing except in answer to questions. He thought this admonition strange, and waited anxiously.

Dr. Eck—not the debater of Leipzig fame but the

representative of the archbishop's court—pointed to a group of books on a central table. He asked Luther if these books were his and if he would recant of the positions set forth in them.

This was too sudden for Luther. He had thought, as Charles' summons had indicated, that this was to be a hearing, not a demand. He seemed powerless to answer. Jerome Schurf, his friend and lawyer, stepped to his rescue, crying out, "Let the titles of the books be read."

They were read. *"To the Christian Nobility of the German Nation! On the Babylonish Captivity of the Church! The Freedom of the Christian Man! . . ."*

By the time the reading was over, Luther had recovered his presence. He was not to be driven too quickly. This was his hour.

He spoke slowly:

His Imperial Majesty asks me two things: first, whether these books are mine, and secondly, whether I will stand by them or recant part of what I have published. First, the books are mine; I deny none of them. The second question, whether I will reassert all or recant what is said to have been written without warrant of Scripture, concerns faith and the salvation of souls and the Divine Word, than which nothing is greater in heaven or in earth, and which we all ought to reverence. Therefore it would be rash and dangerous to say anything without due consideration, since I might say more than the thing demands or less than the truth, either of which would bring me in danger of the sentence of Christ. "Whosoever shall deny me before men, him will I also deny before my Father which is in heaven." Wherefore, I humbly beg your Imperial Majesty to grant me time for deliberation, that I may answer without injury to the Divine Word, or peril to my soul.

Confusion followed for a moment. Charles conferred with his counselors and then with Dr. Eck. Finally Eck addressed Luther:

Although, Martin, you knew from the imperial mandate why you were summoned and therefore you do not deserve to have a longer time given you, yet his Imperial Majesty of his great clemency, grants you one day more, commanding that you appear tomorrow at this time and deliver your answer orally and not in writing.

Luther withdrew from the hall and returned to his rooms. The experience was exacting. For a moment it had looked bad for him. His enemies had almost succeeded in forcing too hasty a statement. Now he knew the question—and he would be ready.

That night, greatly excited, he wrote to a friend: "This hour I have stood before the Emperor and the Diet, asked whether I would revoke my books. . . . Truly, with Christ's aid I shall not retract one jot or tittle."

He was in prayer much of the night. In the morning,

friend after friend came to visit. Luther was in the best of spirits. He was well and strong, laughed heartily, and was in constant good humor. With his intimate associates he planned the work of the afternoon, and he was ready when at four o'clock the herald came. Again through gardens they reached the palace entrance. There they stood in the hot, pressing crowd for an hour and a half.

His mind was fastened rigidly to its one great task. Life was precious to him. His enemies were strong. They might march him easily from the hall of the diet to the stake of Hus. He knew Rome had pleaded with Charles not to keep the promise of safe conduct. But here was his real and valid opportunity to confess his truth before the world. A strange mingling of faith, fear, strength, and exaltation possessed him. And his mind was clear: He would be honest!

At six the emperor and court entered. Aleander and Caracciolo would not come; they said they would not listen to a heretic! Luther entered, cheered by German knights and soldiers.

The session again was conducted by Dr. Eck. He turned to Luther, both men standing, and said:

His Imperial Majesty has assigned this time to you, Martin Luther, to answer for the books which you yesterday openly acknowledged to be yours. You asked time to deliberate on the question whether you would take back part of what you had said or would stand by all of it. You did not deserve this respite, which has now come to an end, for you knew long before why you were sum-

moned. And everyone—especially a professor
of theology—ought to be so certain of his faith
that whenever questioned about it he can give
a sure and positive answer. Now at last reply
to the demand of his Majesty, whose clemency you have experienced in obtaining time
to deliberate. Do you wish to defend all of
your books or to retract part of them?

Luther was self-possessed. He had gained the hour of
his life. He spoke to the greatest assembly of princes
Germany could muster. This was no persecuted plead-
ing, but a clear appeal, in ancient prophetic fervor:

Most Serene Emperor, Most Illustrious
Princes, Most Clement Lords! At the time
fixed yesterday I obediently appear, begging
for the mercy of God, that your Most Serene
Majesty and your illustrious lordships may
deign to hear this cause which I hope may be
called the cause of justice and truth, with
clemency, and if, by my inexperience, I
should fail to give anyone the titles due him,
or should sin against the etiquette of the
court, please forgive me, as a man who has
lived not in courts but in monastic nooks, one
who can say nothing for himself, but that he
has hitherto tried to teach and to write but
with a sincere mind and single eye to the
glory of God and the edification of Christians.
Most Serene Emperor, Most Illustrious
Princes! Two questions were asked me yester-

day. To the first, whether I would recognize that the books published under my name were mine, I gave plain answer, to which I hold and will hold forever, namely, that the books are mine, as I published them, unless perchance it may have happened that the guile or meddlesome wisdom of my opponents has changed something in them. For I only recognize what has been written by myself alone, and not the interpretation added by another.

In reply to the second question, I beg your Most Sacred Majesty and your lordships to be pleased to consider that all my books are not of the same kind. In some I have treated piety, faith, and morals so simply and evangelically that my adversaries themselves are forced to confess that these books are useful, innocent, and worthy to be read by Christians. Even the bull, though fierce and cruel, states that some things in my books are harmless, although it condemns them by a judgment simply monstrous. If, therefore, I should undertake to recant these, would it not happen that I alone of all men should damn the truth which all—friends and enemies alike—confess?

Luther spoke calmly, in complete command of himself, but his deep intensity stilled every noise in the hall. He was being heard clearly.

The second class of my works inveighs against the papacy as against that which both by precept and example has laid waste all Christendom, body and soul. No one can deny or dissemble this fact, since general complaints witness that the consciences of all believers are snared, harassed, and tormented by the laws of the pope and the doctrines of men, and especially that the goods of this famous German nation have been and are devoured in numerous and ignoble ways. Yet the Canon Law provides that the laws and doctrines of the pope contrary to the Gospel and the fathers are to be held erroneous and rejected. If, therefore, I should withdraw these books, I would add strength to tyranny and open windows and doors to their impiety, which would then flourish and burgeon more freely than it ever dared before. It would come to pass that their wickedness would go unpunished, and therefore, would become more licentious on account of my recantation, and their government of the people, thus confirmed and established, would become intolerable, especially if they could boast that I had recanted with the full authority of your Sacred and Most Serene Majesty and of the whole Roman Empire. Good God! In that case, I would be the tool of iniquity and tyranny.

The sound of his voice uplifted in rebuke to high sin

brought a welcome thrill to many a heart. Men forgot the heat and smoke. The defense continued:

> In a third sort of book I have written against some private individuals who tried to defend the Roman tyranny and tear down my pious doctrine. In these I confess I was more bitter than is becoming to a minister of religion. For I do not pose as a saint, nor do I discuss my life but the doctrine of Christ. Yet neither is it right for me to recant what I have said in these, for then tyranny and impiety would rage and reign against the people of God more violently than ever by reason of my acquiescence.

Luther paused a moment, then picked up a triumphant strain, moving in prophetic humility from rebuke to proof, and calling on all present to rise and answer him.

> As I am a man and not God, I wish to claim no other defense for my doctrine than that which the Lord Jesus put forward when he was questioned before Annas and smitten by a servant: He then said, "If I have spoken evil, bear witness of the evil." If the Lord Himself, who knew that He could not err, did not scorn to hear testimony against His doctrine from a miserable servant, how much more should I, the dregs of men, who can do nothing but err, seek and hope that someone should bear witness against my doctrine? I

therefore beg by God's mercy that if your Majesty or your illustrious lordships, from the highest to the lowest, can do it, you should bear witness and convict me of error and conquer me by proofs drawn from the Gospels or the prophets, for I am most ready to be instructed and when convinced will be the first to throw my books into the fire.

From this I think it is sufficiently clear that I have carefully considered and weighed the discords, perils, emulation, and dissension excited by my teaching, concerning which I was gravely and urgently admonished yesterday. To me the happiest side of the whole affair is that the Word of God is made the object of emulation and dissent. For this is the course, the fate, and the result of the Word of God. As Christ says, "I am come not to send peace, but a sword, to set a man against his father and a daughter against her mother." We must consider that our God is wonderful and terrible in His counsels. If we should begin to heal our dissensions by damning the Word of God, we should only turn loose an intolerable deluge of woes.

He spoke now to the heads of the empire. From authority born in Scripture and conscience, he called on the lords of Germany in terms no underling could use. Spaniards and Germans watched the gestureless monk in the uncertain, hot light and heard, unbelieving:

Let us take care that the rule of this excellent youth, Prince Charles (in whom, next God, there is much hope), does not begin inauspiciously. For I could show by many examples drawn from Scripture that when Pharaoh and the King of Babylon and the kings of Israel thought to pacify and strengthen their kingdoms by their own wisdom, they really only ruined themselves. For he taketh the wise in their own craftiness and removeth mountains and they know it not. We must fear God. I do not say this as though your lordships needed either my teaching or my admonition, but because I could not shirk the duty I owed Germany. With these words I commend myself to your Majesty and your lordships, humbly begging that you will not let my enemies make me hateful to you without cause. I have spoken.

In proper custom, he spoke in Latin. Many of the northerners did not understand it, and there were cries for it in German. The hall was hot, Luther perspiring. He seemed on the point of collapse. A Saxon, Frederick von Thun, called out, "If you can't do it, Doctor, you've done enough."

Luther repeated it in German. But Charles V, in whose hands was the destiny of Europe, understood neither Latin nor German! And Leo X, master of the church, who alone had power sufficient for this healing, was far away.

Eck rose, amazed that Luther would dare to speak this

way, and said:

> Luther, you have not answered to the point.
> You ought not to call in question what has
> been decided and condemned by councils.
> Therefore I beg you to give a simple, unso-
> phisticated answer without horns. Will you
> recant or not?

Luther, realizing the point had been called for sharply, said briefly and exactly:

> Since your Majesty and your lordships ask
> for a plain answer, I will give you one without
> either horns or teeth. Unless I am convinced
> by Scripture or by right reason—for I trust
> neither in popes nor in councils, since they
> have often erred and contradicted them-
> selves—unless I am thus convinced, I am
> bound by the texts of the Bible; my con-
> science is captive to the Word of God. I
> neither can nor will recant anything, since it
> is neither right nor safe to act against con-
> science. God help me. Amen.

Eck, furious, called again for recantation. Luther re-plied, while the tumult increased. Charles V rose abruptly and left the room, signifying an end of the audience. The marshal took Luther quickly from the hall, while the Germans cheered and the Spaniards hissed. Fearing an attempt on his life, friends gathered in a marching circle around him. With hands held high in an old Saxon sign of victory, they escorted him through the crowds who jammed the palace court and streets.

Back in his rooms, Luther clapped his hands and shouted happily, "I am through! I am through!"

But he wasn't.

Friends gathered around Luther in the hotel that night, overjoyed with his strong stand at the diet. The Elector Frederick was greatly pleased and remarked to Spalatin how well his Dr. Martin had spoken at the diet that day.

Affairs in the political realm were so tense that the counselors of Frederick and the emperor tried hard to arrive at a compromise. They called on Luther several times during the succeeding few days, but he was adamant. If any compromise involved the surrender of his position, then it was impossible. He had taken his position in public on his conscience. As he saw it, the authority upon which that conscience based its decision was the written word of God. In this field, compromise was out of the question.

In despair, the intermediaries gave up.

Feeling no longer needed in Worms and wanting to get far away before the safe conduct would expire, Luther silently slipped out on the morning of April 26, in the company of the same few friends with whom he had come. The imperial herald, Sturm, did not ride with him for fear of attracting too much attention, but met the party a few miles to the north.

five

Storm

HIGH ABOVE EISENACH
1521-1522

*T*HE JOURNEY HOME was more leisurely and not filled with the anxiety the journey southward had known. Coming into Eisenach, Luther visited his relatives in Mohra. His father's brother Heinz Luther entertained him overnight, and Luther preached the next day in the village. Back in the field and forest of his family, Luther relaxed some from the severe experiences of the past few months and visited many friends and relatives in and around Eisenach.

He resumed his journey May 4. Riding with relatives along a narrow road through the forest, he was surprised by a company of armed horsemen. They forced his carriage to stop, assured the companions no harm was meant, and whispered something to Luther. He turned to his friends and told them he had to leave, but all was well and he would write to them soon. Luther mounted, and off they galloped through the forest.

After a hard ride through the day and well into the

night, they arrived at the castle of Wartburg, where Luther was turned over to the commandant.

Word spread rapidly that Luther had been kidnapped. The little that was known about the affair was told by the eyewitnesses, but no one knew who the kidnappers were or why the deed had been done. Rumor said Luther had been killed. Albrecht Dürer heard the rumor and lamented the death of "the saintly man." He called on Erasmus to take up the leadership and seek the martyr's crown. But Erasmus was not made for martyrdom.

Aleander heard the news and reported to Rome, "Some say that I have had him killed, others the Archbishop of Mayence. Would God it were true!"

The secret of his disappearance was guarded rigidly. Suspicions that the Elector Frederick had a hand in it could not be proved, and no one except a few in the intimate circle had any idea what had happened. To reassure some of his most intimate friends, Luther wrote them after a few weeks to tell them of his health and safety, but he did not divulge his hiding place. The Elector Frederick was afraid Luther would be assassinated, as the Romanists wished. In all probability, the plans for this ruse were laid in the emperor's own private chambers, with only Spalatin and a few others aware of them.

Luther himself was taken by surprise, but he was quickly reassured at Wartburg. There he was treated as a guest, with respect and honor. Hidden now from the world of turmoil, he lived as one set apart from that world. He dressed as a knight and was spoken to by everyone as "Sir George." Thick black hair appeared over his tonsure, and a full beard covered his chin.

The first few weeks of his hiding passed quickly and quietly. Then the old restlessness repossessed him. He had been born, it seems, for battle, and for ten long years he had been moving steadily in public warfare. The great desire of his mind and heart was to give what he called "evangelical leadership" to the people of Saxony.

And so in his room in the Wartburg, undisturbed by the routine duties of professorship and parish, he set his fine abilities to a task he long had anticipated. He would translate his beloved New Testament into the German language. Many German translations were available, but each was in dialect. He would set forth the blessed stories so they could be understood generally.

Throughout the long summer months and well into the winter he labored at these tasks. Not only did the New Testament translation progress in the Wartburg; there also came from his pen tract after tract on all the major issues of the controversy. He wrote sermons on the Gospels and Epistles to be used in the regular cycle of the church year. He wrote on the Mass and on monastic vows.

As he wrote on monastic vows, with much time for reflection, the old controversy between himself and his father, when he had taken his own vows, came to mind. He could see now, as he could not see then, something intrinsically wrong in the Roman practice with regard to vows. The deep piety of his father was clearer to him. He could understand now how piety and resistance to the organization could be united in one person. When the book was ready for the public, Martin wrote to Hans:

The Wilderness
November 21, 1521

This book, dear father, I wish to dedicate to you, not to make your name famous in the world, for fame puffeth up the flesh, according to the doctrine of St. Paul, but that I might have occasion in a short preface as it were between you and me to point out to the Christian reader the argument and contents of the book, together with an illustrative example. . . .

It is now sixteen years since I became a monk, having taken the vow without your knowledge and against your will. You were anxious and fearful about my weakness, because I was a young blood of twenty-two; that is, to use St. Augustine's words, it was still hot youth with me, and you had learned from numerous examples that monkery made many unblessed and so were determined to marry me honorably and tie me down. This fear, this anxiety, this nonconsent of yours were for a time simply irreconcilable.

And, indeed, my vow was not worth a fig, since it was taken without the consent of the parents God gave me. Moreover it was a godless vow both because taken against your will and without my whole heart. In short, it was simple doctrine of men; that is, of the spiritual state of hypocrites, a doctrine not commanded by God. . . .

Dear father, will you still take me out of the cloister? If so, do not boast of it, for God has anticipated you and taken me out himself. What *difference does it make whether I retain or lay aside the cowl and the tonsure? Do they make the monk? . . . My conscience is free and redeemed; therefore I am still a monk but not a monk, and a new creature not of the Pope, but of Christ, for the Pope also has creatures and is a creator of puppets and idols and masks and straw men, of which I was formerly one, but now have escaped by the Word. . . .*

The Pope may strangle me and condemn me and bid me go to Hell, but he will not be able to rouse me after death to strangle me again. To be banned and damned is according to my own heart and will. May he never absolve me more! I hope the great day is at hand when the kingdom of abomination and horror will be broken and thrust down. Would to God that I had been worthy to be burned by the Pope! . . .

The Lord bless you, dear father, with mother, your Margaret, and all our family. Farewell in the Lord Christ.

He treated the problem of vows as he did everything else, asking only one question: "What does Scripture say?" From Scripture he argued vows were hostile to the good of Christianity. He strongly cut away the basis for the great monastic emphasis on celibacy. The Bible encourages marriage, does not place a greater premium on virginity, and destroys the distinction between clergy and laity.

The book was widely read and very influential. Once again it touched a source of income for Albert, Archbishop of Mayence, for he sold licenses to priests to permit them to keep concubines. Marriage of the clergy assumed an important phase of the struggle after the appearance of this book.

There were many lovely incidents during his Wartburg stay. The hills around the castle, familiar to him since school days in Eisenach, were the scene of many walks. He tried to live the life of knight and hunter and took part in the chase, but his mind did not function well there. He always derived some theological analogy from the hunt. His heart was too tender and gentle to enjoy the snared rabbit. But the flowers and the same fields which had delighted the eye of his childhood were now his joy.

His life was centered, however, in the moments in his room when all the strength of his nature was concentrated on religious study. Superstitious as always, he now had time to nurse his superstition. Unbothered by routine duties, he could hear through the long hours of silence strange noises throughout the old castle. As always, when a direct cause could not be seen for action, he associated the action with the devil or the Holy Spirit. So he heard the devil in strange noises in his room, under his bed, outside the door. He moved quickly to scare the devil from behind a chair, or flung his ink bottle to crash to pieces on the opposite wall.

It is no wonder he should imagine the devil plagued him, leered at him from across the room, and laughed at him when the Greek would not respond during his studies. With his strong, impetuous nature, he had been so active during the past five years and now was forced to inaction, concentrating on Greek and Hebrew grammar, wrestling with New Testament phrases to bring them into his beloved German language. No wonder, either, that fury possessed him when he thought of the way Rome had handled the precious Gospel and himself, its proclaimer.

As he sat in Wartburg, Archbishop Albert was displaying at Halle 9,000 relics, including manna from the wilderness, the burning bush of Moses, and jars from the wedding at Cana, with the promise of indulgence for those who came. Albert also was reopening the indulgence sale. Against this abuse Luther wrote a terrible pamphlet titled "The Idol of Halle." He gave it to Spalatin to print, but Spalatin showed it to Frederick, and Luther was urged not to publish it. However, Luther wrote a powerful letter to Albert, demanding once again that Albert cease the abusive practices:

To Albert, Archbishop and Elector of Mayence:
[The Wartburg] December 1, 1521

My humble servant to your Electoral Grace,
my honorable and gracious Lord. Your Grace
doubtless remembers vividly that I have written
you twice before, the first time at the beginning of
the indulgence fraud protected by your Grace's
name. In that letter I faithfully warned your
Grace and from Christian love set myself against
those deceitful, seducing, greedy preachers
thereof, and against their heretical, infidel books.
Had I not preferred to act with moderation I
might have driven the whole storm on your Grace
as the one who aided and abetted the traders,
and I might have written expressly against their

heretical books, but instead I spared your Grace and the house of Brandenburg, thinking that your Grace might have acted through ignorance, led astray by false whisperers, so I only attacked them, and with how much trouble and danger as your Grace knows.

But as this my true admonition was mocked by your Grace, obtaining ingratitude instead of thanks, I wrote you a second time (Feb. 4, 1520) humbly asking for information. To this I got a hard, improper, unepiscopal, unchristian answer (Feb. 26, 1520), referring me to higher powers for information. As these two letters did no good, I am now sending your Grace a third warning, according to the Gospel, this time in German, hoping that such admonition and prayer, which ought to be superfluous and unnecessary, may help.

Your Grace has again erected at Halle that idol which robs poor simple Christians of their money and their souls. You have thus shown that the criminal blunder for which Tetzel was blamed was not due to him alone, but also to the Arch-bishop of Mayence, who, not regarding my gentleness to him, insists on taking all the blame on himself. Perhaps your Grace thinks I am no more to be reckoned with, but am looking out for my own safety, and that his Imperial Majesty has extinguished the poor monk. On the contrary, I wish Your Grace to know that I will do what Christian love demands without fearing the gates of hell, much less unlearned popes, bishops, and

*cardinals. I will not suffer it nor keep silence
when the Archbishop of Mayence gives out that it
is none of his business to give information to a
poor man who asks for it. The truth is that your
ignorance is wilful, as long as the thing ignored
brings you in money. I am not to blame, but your
own conduct.*

Luther was in earnest. His mind worked clearly and
quickly. His sentences cut through to the issue every
time. He heard the roar of the Lion of Amos and could not
keep silent.

*I humbly pray your Grace, therefore, to leave
poor people undeceived and unrobbed, and show
yourself a bishop rather than a wolf. It has been
made clear enough that indulgences are only
knavery and fraud, and that only Christ should
be preached to the people, so that your Grace has
not the excuse of ignorance. Your Grace will
please remember the beginning, and what a
terrible fire was kindled from a little despised
spark, and how all the world was surely of the
opinion that a single poor beggar was immeasur-
ably too weak for the Pope, and was undertaking
an impossible task. But God willed to give the
Pope and his followers more than enough to do,
and to play a game contrary to the expectation of
the world, and in spite of it, so that the Pope will
hardly recover, growing daily worse, and one
may see God's hand therein. Let no one doubt
that the same God yet lives and knows how to*

*withstand a cardinal of Mayence even if four
emperors would support him. . . .*

Strange things had been done by the power of God, and
Luther was certain that in this cause emperors were no
match for the Holy Spirit. He took upon himself the
prophet's authority and delivered an ultimatum to the
cardinal:

*Wherefore I write to tell your Grace that if the
idol is not taken down, my duty to godly doctrine
and Christian salvation will absolutely force me
to attack your Grace publicly as I did the Pope,
and oppose your undertaking, and lay all the
odiums which Tetzel once had, on the Archbishop of Mayence, and show all the world the
difference between a bishop and a wolf. . . .
Moreover, I beg your Grace to leave in peace the
priests who, to avoid unchastity, have betaken
themselves to marriage. Do not deprive them of
their God-given rights. Your Grace has no authority, reason, nor right to persecute them, and
arbitrary crime does not become a bishop. . . . So
your Grace can see that if you do not take care,
the Evangelic party will raise an outcry and point
out that it would become a bishop first to cast the
beam out of his own eye and put away his harlots
before he separates pious wives from their husbands. . . .
I will not keep silence, for, though I do not
expect it, I hope to make the bishops leave off
singing their lively little song. . . .*

I beg and expect a right speedy answer from your Grace within the next fortnight, for at the expiration of that time my pamphlet against the Idol of Halle will be published unless a proper answer comes. And if this letter is received by your Grace's secretaries and does not come into your own hands, I will not hold off for that reason. Secretaries should be true and a bishop should so order his court that that reaches him which should reach him. God give your Grace His grace unto a right mind and will.

Your Grace's obedient, humble servant,

Martin Luther

Luther's letter was dated December 1. Before the end of the month a messenger brought to the Wartburg a letter addressed to "Martin Luther, in care of Spalatin." Luther opened it and read:

Halle, December 21, 1521

My dear doctor, I have received your letter and I take it in good part and graciously, and will see to it that the thing that moved you so be done away, and I will act, God willing, as becomes a pious, spiritual, and Christian prince, as far as God gives me grace and strength, for which I earnestly pray and have prayers said for me, for I can do nothing of myself, and know well that without God's grace there is no good in me, but that I am as much foul mud as any other, if not

*more. I do not wish to conceal this, for I am
more than willing to show you grace and favor
for Christ's sake, and I can well bear fraternal
and Christian punishment. I hope the merciful,
kind God will give me herein more grace,
strength, and patience to live in this matter and
in others by his will.*

Albert, with his own hand

It was not easy for Luther to remain out of leadership in the most crucial days of the new movement. He thought with bitterness and scorn of the tricks to which Aleander and Charles V had resorted at Worms. He read the Edict of Worms, calling on the people of Germany to surrender him for his proper condemnation, with a warning to all who gave him shelter, food, or clothes or who read, bought, sold, or printed any of his books. He paced back and forth through the halls of Wartburg, impatient at Frederick's continued demand for his seclusion.

There were days in the Wartburg when his gifts of clear exposition were at their height and he felt himself working with the highest efficiency. But on other days all the distractions and balked fury of these years of quarreling got the better of him.

Impatient, restless for leadership, he finally was permitted by Frederick to come out of his seclusion by the course of events at Wittenberg. There, in his absence, colleagues like Andrew Bodenstein were moving too rapidly. They wanted to throw over the entire ancient organization and faith. Luther, by nature and training, was thoroughly conservative. He had been driven by life's severest experiences to open up the abuses in his church, but he devoutly loved the church itself, and he would keep all its ancient customs. Not so the more radical men who had welcomed his leadership. Wittenberg needed him badly.

He had corresponded with his friends all winter and knew the situation exactly. Melanchthon pleaded with him to return. Finally, in the spring of 1522, he quietly slipped away from the Wartburg. Still with a beard and full head of hair, dressed as a knight and with a sword by his side, he journeyed incognito through the territory of Duke George of Saxony—who willingly would have turned him over to the authorities, had he caught him. Though warned of the duke's intention, Luther had written that he would come through Leipzig to Wittenberg "though it should rain Duke Georges for nine days in succession, each fiercer than the other." Through Erfurt, Jena, and Leipzig, "Sir George" traveled toward Wittenberg.

In an inn at Jena one night, two students noticed a strange contradiction between the sword by the side of the knight and the book the knight was reading: the Psalms in Hebrew. Well-informed on the movements of the Reformation, the students talked with the knight and surmised he was Luther. One of them described him in a letter and noted that he was "somewhat stout, yet upright, bending backward rather than stooping, with deep, dark eyes and eyebrows, twinkling and sparkling like stars, so that one could hardly look steadily at them."

No one but the two Swiss students suspected his identity, and he arrived safely at Wittenberg. He talked with Melanchthon and his other friends and analyzed the situation with them. Then for eight successive days he preached in the village church against the fanatical activities that had resulted in the destruction of pictures and images and in the breakdown of organizational morale.

At the close of the week he was once again the leader of the Wittenberg movement. The radical wing of the Reformation would locate its center elsewhere.

Luther turned his attention to explaining and defending his cause. One of the first matters that engaged him on his return to Wittenberg was the pamphlet written by King Henry VIII of England in answer to Luther's *On the Babylonian Captivity of the Church.* Erasmus had spoken to Henry of Luther in 1520, asking the king's favorable interest. But Cardinal Wolsey was more influential than Erasmus and succeeded in focusing Henry's thought on the destructive phases of Luther's work. The cardinal gave the king a copy of Luther's "Babylonian Captivity" and suggested Henry answer it. Henry did so in July 1521, while Luther was in the Wartburg. Henry's work was called An Assertion of the Seven Sacraments and was dedicated to Pope Leo X.

He did not handle Luther gently. As a matter of fact, no polemical work of the early sixteenth century treated its enemy kindly. The language was powerful with disgust and abuse: "What pest so pernicious as Luther has ever attacked the flock of Christ? What a wolf of hell he is! What a limb of Satan!"

These and similar expressions prompted Leo X to confer upon the king of England the title "The Defender of the Faith." (Within fifteen years, Henry would earn his title!) Luther read the book and responded in an exceptionally violent attack on Henry. His pamphlet, printed in July 1522, branded its adversary "That king of lies, King Henry, by God's ungrace, King of England." Years later, Luther would offer an apology for the severity of his words when he heard the king of England himself was deserting the Roman communion. But for now, Henry and his English counselors were numbered among Luther's deadliest enemies.

Luther, with Melanchthon's help, now concentrated on the clear formulation of the Wittenberg position. Throughout 1520 and 1521, Melanchthon had worked on an outline of theology constructed from Paul's letter to the Romans. He had sent a copy to Luther at the Wartburg. Now, with Luther's approval, he published it in Wittenberg, calling it *Loci Communes Rerum Theologicarum* ("Theological Commonplaces"). It moved in the evangelic circle of ideas, beginning with the doctrine of the Trinity and then setting forth the idea of "Man, Sin, The Law, The Gospel, Grace, Faith, The Sacraments, The Magistracy, Church Government, Condemnation, and Blessedness."

Such a logical, systematic presentation was needed, and Melanchthon's detailed skill was equal to the task. The proofs of argument were all scriptural, and the book marked a tremendous advance for the Luther forces.

Far away in his retreat at Salzburg, Staupitz watched Luther's progress with both sorrow and joy. He had loved the sensitive, enthusiastic boy who had come to the Augustinian monastery at Erfurt in 1505. Augustinian? The old vicar-general meditated on the changes of life that had driven him from the order he loved to take refuge, by papal arrangement, with the Benedictines, while the young monk, now mature, battled for piety in the open world.

The last exchange of letters between the two old friends was in 1523-24, after the great crisis in the battle had passed. Luther wrote in September 1523:

> *Reverend Father in Christ, your silence is most unjust, and you know that we are obliged to think of it. But even if you are no longer pleased with me, it is not fitting that I should forget you, who first made the light of the Gospel to shine in my heart.*

This called forth the last letter, dated April 1, 1524, from Salzburg:

> *My love to you is most constant, passing the love of women, always unbroken. . . . But as I do not grasp all of your ideas, I keep silence with them. . . . But we owe much to you, Martin, for having led us back from the husks which the swine did eat to the pastures of life and the words of salvation.*

Staupitz died in December 1524.

THE WHIRLWIND
1525

The severest test Luther ever had to face came in 1524–

25, during the so-called "Peasants' Revolt." The causes of the revolt lay deep in human history, completely disconnected from the Reformation.

"The long, long patience of the plundered poor" is, as Edwin Markham said, a constant wonder. For centuries in central Europe the peasant class had been ruled strictly by both civil and ecclesiastical nobles. The long story of uprisings to gain their birthright is told throughout history.

In the German area where Luther was called upon to face the movement, these uprisings had become increasingly severe and frequent during the 150 years preceding 1525. The leaders of the church were more at fault than those of the laity. For centuries, bishops and other high church officials had kept serfs in severe oppression.

Two sources contributed to the peasant rebellion throughout these years: first, the refusal of the oppressed classes to bear oppression beyond a certain point, and second, the preaching of the New Testament. The same church that reared and owned ecclesiastical princes preserved in other priests the strange Gospel message of equality.

Long before Luther, these two streams of rebellion and the Gospel had met in the forests of central Germany. The "Bundschuh" was a secret society dedicated to social rebellion. Its symbol was the peasant's shoe—tied, in token of servility, instead of buckled, as were the shoes of the nobility. When this symbol was carried through the country on Bundschuh banners, it stirred tremendous feeling and instilled strong allegiance. Great preachers of the social Gospel like Hans Boheim inspired the peasants' efforts.

In a sense, history seems to be an endless war between the oppressed and the more favored classes. The peasants would gather strength for a century and break into rebellion, only to be beaten back by superior technique and equipment. Then they would nurse their wrath for generations until again, sorely pressed, they stormed the princes' castles.

Now, in the volatile days of the late fifteenth and early sixteenth centuries, there was a groundswell of rebellion throughout central Europe. The papacy, ancient symbol of autocratic strength, was weakening and fighting for its hold on Europe. The Holy Roman Empire was no longer the source of strength it once had been, and many princes were refusing allegiance to their chief. Feudalism was in its last stages. Francis I in France, Henry VIII in England, Charles V in Spain, Caesar Borgia in Italy, and Julius II in Rome all acted from personal will, in violent disregard of human rights and accepted medieval law. Wealth increasingly was concentrated in the hands of the few, stolen from the many. Luxury and its ever-present companions, immorality and brutality, spread through Europe's armed classes. Hundreds of the finest minds of Christendom attacked from all angles the abuse in recognized authority.

The day after Luther left Worms, Magellan had been killed in the Philippines. During the early months of Luther's stay in the Wartburg, Cortés had accomplished his dastardly conquest of Mexico, with the death of Montezuma. The European peasants moved in perfect rhythm with this transforming and reforming world. This was their hour to strike. The restless movement grew steadily—unfortunately led by men unequipped for the task.

The crisis came late in 1524. The countess of Lupfen, whose estate bordered Lake Constance, attempted to force her serfs to gather snail shells for guests at the castle. It was a church holiday on which the serfs were not obligated to work. In response to her whim, they rose in rebellion. The entire Swabian peasantry joined the outbreak. It spread northward, terrorizing the people.

A young count, von Helfenstein, married to the daughter of the late Emperor Maximilian and safe—he thought—in his castle near Weinsberg, was particularly arrogant. He cut the throats of some peasants he met on the road one day. A large force of peasants led by "Little Jack" Rohrbach besieged his castle. Helfenstein offered ransom but was refused. He surrendered and was led out between two lines of peasants with pikes pointed inward. His wife, with a baby in her arms, begged for mercy. A piper mockingly played a death dance as the lines of pikes closed in.

One month later, after a bloody encounter, the nobles captured some of the peasants who had taken the Helfenstein castle, including the man who had piped the dance. They chained the piper to an apple tree and lit a fire around the tree. Slowly he roasted, jumping from point to point, shrieking while his tormentors drank and sang lustily.

Thomas Munzer, who at Zwickau had organized a fanatical sect dedicated to church and state reform, assumed a precarious leadership throughout these years. He had been driven from Zwickau and Wittenberg. After a hazardous existence in many cities, he had established his leadership in the town of Muhlhausen. There he preached a violent rebellion, claiming this was the hour when the Holy Spirit would lead the peasants to their rightful reward. He himself was unbalanced, hasty, and ignorant, but moved by a fiery spirit. His father had been killed brutally by nobles. He urged the peasants to strike for the biblical "promised land" and assured them legions of angels would fight for them.

Munzer offered the German peasants vicious advice: "Arise! Fight the battle of the Lord! On! On! On! Now is the time. The wicked tremble when they hear you. Be pitiless! Heed not the groans of the impious! Rouse up the towns and villages! Above all, rouse up the miners of the mountains! On! On! On while the fire is burning! On while the sword is yet reeking with the slaughter! Give the fire no time to go out, the sword no time to cool! Kill all the proud ones; while one of them lives you will not be free from the fear of men. While they reign over you it is no use to talk of God."

As the movement spread violently northward into Saxony, it became increasingly clear Luther had to speak. This was no child's play. It was the opening of the rebellion. During the summer of 1524, the peasants were successful everywhere. When they captured a castle or an estate, they robbed, pillaged, and murdered without restraint. The torch and the sword, with all the accompanying hideousness to which a human mob can descend, rose menacingly above Germany.

Luther's mind was clear. He was thoroughly conservative in civil affairs. Never in his life had he sanctioned force, except by the civil magistrate. He would have died unresisting at Worms, had they led him to the stake. He would never have approved an armed defense by the

Elector Frederick and Saxon warriors on his behalf.

On his return from the Wartburg to Wittenberg in 1522, during the memorable week of preaching in which he had stilled the revolution there, he had said:

> I will preach, speak, write, but I will force no one; for faith must be voluntary. Take me as an example. I stood up against the Pope, indulgences, and all the papists, but without violence or uproar. I only urged, preached, and declared God's Word, nothing else. And yet while I was asleep, or with my Philip Melanchthon and Amsdorf, the word inflicted greater injury on popery than prince or emperor ever did. I did nothing; the Word did everything. Had I appealed to force, all Germany might have been deluged with blood. Yes, I might have kindled a conflict at Worms, so that the emperor would not have been safe. But what would have been the result? Ruin and desolation of body and soul. I therefore kept quiet, and gave the Word free course through the world. Do you know what the devil thinks when he sees men use violence to propagate the Gospel? He sits with folded arms behind the fire of hell, and says with malignant looks and frightful grin: "Ah, how wise these madmen are to play my game! Let them go on; I shall reap the benefit. I delight in it." But when he sees the Word running and contending alone on the battlefield, then he shudders and shakes for fear.

The Word is almighty, and takes captive the hearts.

His heart was ever a peasant's heart. The blood in his veins, he boasted, was peasant blood. No one in Europe had spoken more directly against the abuses of the ruling class than he, and now he faced the strange, terrible conflict between his native, idealistic sympathy for the peasants and his strong belief in the divine order of civil government. The princes he had known in Saxony, chiefly the Elector Frederick, had been wise and well controlled. But in this hour when the uprising was at its height, Frederick was on his deathbed and could not organize his followers to the defense.

Luther was in hearty sympathy with the peasants' demands. The peasant leaders had stated their position in the famous Twelve Articles, drawn up during the winter of 1524–25 and adopted in a council at Memmingen on March 7. Luther read these carefully:

1. The right to choose their own pastors.

2. They would pay tithe of corn, out of which the pastors should be paid, the rest going to the use of the parish. But small tithes, i.e., of the produce of animals, every tenth calf, or pig, or egg, and so on, they would not pay.

3. They would be free, and no longer serfs and bondmen.

4. Wild game and fish are to be free to all.

5. Woods and forests belong to all for fuel.

6. No services of labor to be more than were required of their forefathers.

7. If more service required, wages must be paid for it.

8. Rent, when above the value of the land, to be properly valued and lowered.

9. Punishments for crimes to be fixed.

10. Common land to be given up again to common use.

11. Death gifts (i.e., the right of the lord to take the best chattel of the deceased tenant) to be done away with.

12. Any of these articles proved to be contrary to the Scriptures or God's justice, to be null and void.

This, he thought, was clear and honorable. He left Wittenberg, journeyed down through the insurrection areas, visited the peasant camps and in Eisleben wrote his *Exhortation to Peace on the Twelve Articles of the Swabian Peasants.*

In this, he spoke to the nobles:

We need thank no one on earth for this

foolish rebellion but you, my lords, and especially you blind bishops, parsons, and monks, for you, even yet hardened, cease not to rage against the holy Gospel, although you know that our cause is right and you cannot controvert it. Besides this, in civil government you do nothing but oppress and tax to maintain your pomp and pride, until the poor common man neither can nor will bear it longer. The sword is at your throat, and yet you still think you sit so firm in the saddle that no one can hoist you out. You will find out that by such hardened presumption you will break your necks. . . . If these peasants don't do it, others will; God will appoint others, for he intends to smite you and will smite you. . . .

But the prophets of murder are hostile to you as to me, and they have gone among the people these three years and no one has withstood them but I.

He also spoke to the peasants:

It is my friendly and fraternal prayer, dearest brothers, to be very careful what you do. Believe not all spirits and preachers. . . . Those who take the sword shall perish by the sword and every soul should be subject to the powers that be, in fear and honor. . . . If the government is bad and intolerable, that is no excuse for riot and insurrection, for to punish evil belongs not to everyone, but to the civil

> authority which bears the sword. . . . Suffer-
> ing tyranny is a cross given by God.

He believed firmly in the peasants' rights. He also believed in the rights of civil government, and he hoped for arbitration. But it was too late for arbitration. Not even Luther's powerful spirit could check the rising fury of the suicidal struggle. He saw with increasing anguish his country broken, its fields destroyed, cloisters and castles burned, all types of violence and anarchy.

His mind dwelt on the progress of his own great cause. He remembered the Diet of Worms and saw the evangelical faith defended by the princes of northern Germany. He knew how terrible and unchecked was the license of Munzer and the radicals. He knew the hopelessness and helplessness of destructive civil war. He preached in town after town and in the camps of peasants, gathered for war, against this violence. He pleaded for peace. He visited the wounded and plague-stricken in the gathering places of the peasant army.

In Nordhauser, Munzer's friends drowned the sound of Luther's voice by ringing church bells. Yet in Eisleben, Stalberg, Erfurt, Wallhausen, Weimar, and many other towns he continued to strive for peace.

Throughout March and April the situation grew worse. Both Frederick and his brother, who was to succeed him as elector of Saxony, were unable to cope with the uprising. The staunch old elector, ever loyal to his subjects, weakened physically while Luther preached against the revolution. Word came to Luther at Weimar that he was wanted at the deathbed, but it was too late; Frederick died, to Luther's deep sorrow. His strong protector was gone, and rioting was everywhere.

In desperation, angered at the continued resistance of the peasants to his counsels of peace, resting on the old Pauline assertion that they must obey the rulers God had set over them, Luther argued for the relief—not for the destruction—of his people. It was a frightful, bitter hour. He was driven to choose between two evils, sensing anarchy in his native land. In May, he wrote the pamphlet *Against the Thievish, Murderous Hordes of Peasants.*

> In my former book [*Exhortation to Peace*], I dared not judge the peasants, since they asked to be instructed, and Christ says Judge not. But before I could look around they forgot their request and betake themselves to violence—rob, rage, and act like mad dogs, whereby one may see what they had in their false minds, and that their pretense to speak in the name of the Gospel in the Twelve Articles was a simple lie. They do mere devil's work, especially that Satan of Muhlhausen does nothing but rob, murder, and pour out blood.
>
> The peasants have deserved death for three reasons: (1) because they have broken their oath of fealty; (2) for rioting and plundering; and (3) for having covered their terrible sins with the name of the Gospel. Wherefore, my lords, free, save, help, and pity the poor people; stab, smite, and slay all ye that can. If you die in battle you could never have a more blessed end, for you die obedient to God's

Word in Romans 13, and in the service of
love to free your neighbor from the bands of
hell and the devil. I implore everyone who
can to avoid the peasants as he would the
devil himself. I pray God will enlighten them
and turn their hearts. But if they do not turn,
I wish them no happiness for ever more. . . .
Let none think this too hard who considers
how intolerable is rebellion.

His heart was sensitive to peasant and noble alike, but this was an issue of lasting social consequence. He knew the peasant leadership was thoughtless, impractical, without hope of salvation. He was confident in his Saxon princes. He was not deserting the peasant cause; his leadership had never been accepted by the peasants. His Gospel had never undergirded the revolution. The peasants had followed the brutal, insane leadership of men like Munzer—"that Satan of Muhlhausen."

The decisive battle of the revolution was fought near Frankenhausen on May 15. It was terrible. The peasants were equipped with rude weapons—pitchforks, wood axes, scythes, spears, and bows. Across a long, open field they barricaded themselves behind overturned farm wagons and whatever other impediments they could find. Exhorted by Munzer's promises that a miracle would occur, they awaited the attack.

The charge came under the able leadership of the Landgrave Philip of Hesse. Well-armed knights on armored horses, with stout lances and sharp swords, swept all before them. No peasant was alive when the sun went down, except those who had hidden or fled. Thomas

Munzer was executed.

Social darkness settled over Germany. A great cause had been miserably led. The peasants felt hurt that the lion of Wittenberg had not fought with them. All over Europe, the conservative class—men who rationalized their own desires—blamed Luther for the rebellion. They could not see that their miserable, selfish actions over the centuries had stirred up the fury. Had the peasants followed Luther's advice, sought their freedom in the inner life and worked it out in heroic civic exertion, they might have achieved great freedom.

Luther was no coward. He stood his ground. He had worked for the peasants. He would be a peasant until his death. But physical violence was not his to command.

Regardless, against his will and by force of circumstance, the church that bears his name moved from that day closer and closer to the princes, with disastrous consequences.

Commenting on the cause of the revolution, Frederic Seebohm wrote:

> The monks blamed Erasmus and the new learning; Erasmus blamed the wildness of Luther; Luther blamed the wilder prophets. Who was to blame? History will not lay blame on Erasmus, or Luther, or the wilder prophets, or on the misguided peasantry, but on the higher powers whose place it was to have averted revolution by timely reforms. It was their refusal of reform which was the real cause of revolution. It was the conspiracy of the higher powers at the Diet of Worms to

sacrifice the common weal to their own ambi-
tious objects on which history will lay the
blame of the Peasants' War.

The peasant rebellion brought the last argument necessary to force one other break in the ranks of reform. The
humanist group, headed by Erasmus, in the early days
had been jubilant over Luther's leadership. Then, as they
had seen the movement result in a separation from
Rome, one by one they had dropped away, preferring to
stay in the atmosphere of the ancient faith.

Erasmus had been so thoroughly connected with the
reform movement during its origin that a current proverb quipped: "Erasmus laid the egg and Luther hatched
it." Erasmus denied it as historic fact, but he could not
deny the close affiliation between his humanism and
certain phases of Luther's Reformation.

Refusing to follow Luther away from the Catholic
Church, Erasmus felt their paths separating. A man of
finesse in the field of criticism and abuse, he resented
Luther's coarser method. He was angered at the language Luther used toward Henry VIII, who had been
Erasmus' patron. Erasmus always avoided terrible social
upheavals, and he saw the peasant rebellion as being
caused partially, at least, by Luther's unbridled attack on
pope and emperor.

But their final separation came in the field of thought.
The question was the doctrine of free will and predestination. Erasmus published first. He maintained the
doctrine of the freedom of the will, at least to the extent
that the individual must accept the grace of God by his
or her own free will. His pamphlet carried harsh words

against Luther, of course.

Luther gave the matter serious consideration, and after a long interval—for him—he published in December 1525 his reply, *On the Slavery of the Will*. Here his mind is shown moving from religious experience into the problems of thought. The history of the church usually shows that the approach from logic leads to the doctrine of free will, and the approach from religious experience, as such, leads to the doctrine of the absolute will of God. So Luther stated in strong, terse sentences that the human will is devoid of all freedom, that in its sinful, normal state it is ridden by the devil as a human rides a horse. Likewise, in its saved state it is ridden by the Holy Spirit.

The basis of this belief was a firm conviction in the absolute, total sovereignty of God. To permit free will is to deny the power and glory of the creating mind. This is not a thought in which the humanistic mind can rest content. When it became obvious, after the exchange of several pamphlets between Luther and Erasmus, where Luther stood, most of the humanists left his following.

Poor Philip Melanchthon overawed both by Luther's affection and by his strength, was unable to protest to the master himself, but all his life he sympathized with the humanist position.

six

Coloring Leaves

Catharine von Bora
1525

Luther's boyhood in Mansfield had given him a deep and affectionate appreciation of a Christian home. His friendship with Ursula Cotta in Eisenach had strengthened his belief in the essential piety of family life. But any thoughts of a wife and family had been forced to the background when he had taken the vows in the Erfurt monastery in 1505. There is no authentic record that Luther had loved and courted during his young manhood, although he was happy, free, and often in mixed company throughout his student days.

In the Erfurt monastery his great struggle had not against sexual desire or indulgence. He tried to purge his mind of thoughts he considered unworthy of his Christian calling. It had been a long, hard fight, but it had not been a fight against action or a fight to control overpowering passion.

During the opening days of the Reformation, he had moved impersonally through the great disputes. At the Wartburg, writing against monastic vows, he was still as a knight on a battlefield, not a criminal in court. His boyhood home was clearly in his mind when he wrote against the vows.

Back in Wittenberg after the Wartburg seclusion, he found that as a result of his attack on monastic vows, men and women were leaving monastery and convent—some probably from nonevangelical motives, but the great majority for honorable reasons. Many fine thinkers before and after him believed the vows were against the commandments of Scripture.

Luther defended marriage of the clergy on the grounds that it was the first picture of humanity presented in the opening chapters of Genesis. God had created man and woman and had called for their life together. All through the Scriptures, marriage appears as the ideal life. Nowhere in Luther's reading of the Old Testament could he find justification for suspending this relationship. By the laws of nature and the laws of God, the married life is justified.

The Roman Catholic position—a position not shared by the older Greek Catholic Church—based the celibate ideal on the separation of clergy and laity. Luther steadfastly denied this separation, setting forth his famous doctrine of the priesthood of all believers.

So he found only cause for joy when his friends in Wittenberg and other northern German towns, released from their vows by allegiance to the Reformation, began to marry. Philip Melanchthon, Justus Jonas, and other leaders in the movement were established in homes of their own by 1525. Melanchthon, though overawed by the might of Luther, had protested that the cares of married life might inconvenience his studies. But he finally was won over and married the daughter of the chief magistrate of Wittenberg; they lived together for almost half a century in quiet contentment.

The issue took on serious consequences, however, when nuns came to Wittenberg from the convents without economic security, expecting guidance. Among several groups of nuns seeking refuge in Wittenberg came a group of nine in April 1523. Luther wrote to George Spalatin:

Wittenberg, April 10, 1523

Grace and peace. Nine fugitive nuns, a wretched crowd, have been brought to me by honest citizens of Torgau. I mean Leonard Coppe and his nephew, Will Tomitzsch; there is no cause for suspicion. I pity them much, but most of all the others who are dying everywhere in such numbers in their cursed and impure celibacy. This sex, so very, very weak, joined by nature or rather by God to the other, perishes when cruelly separated. O tyrants! O cruel parents and kinsmen in Germany. O Pope and bishops, who can curse you enough? Who can sufficiently execrate the blind fury which has taught and enforced such things? But this is not the place to do it.

You ask what I shall do with them? First I shall inform their relatives and ask them to support the girls; if they will not I shall have the girls otherwise provided for. Some of the families have already promised me to take them; for some I shall get husbands if I can. Their names are

Magdalene von Staupitz, Elsa von Canitz, Ave Gross, Ave von Schonfeld and her sister Margaret, Laneta von Goltz, Margaret and Catharine Zeschau, and Catharine von Bora. Here are they, who serve Christ, in need of true pity. They have escaped from the cloister in miserable condition. I pray you also do the work of charity and beg some money for me from your rich courtiers, by which I can support the girls for a week or two until their kinsmen or others provide for them. For my Capernaans have no wealth but that of the Word, so that I myself could not find the loan of ten gulden for a poor citizen the other day. The poor, who would willingly give, have nothing; the rich either refuse or give so reluctantly that they lose the credit of the gift with God and take up my time begging from them. Nothing is too much for the world and its way. Of my annual salary I have only ten or fifteen gulden left, besides which not a penny has been given me by my brothers or by the city. But I ask them for nothing, to emulate the boast of Paul, despoiling other churches to serve my Corinthians free. . . .

Farewell and pray for me,
Martin Luther

He must have talked with great interest to Magdalene von Staupitz, thinking of the long affection, now strained, between her brother and himself.

One after another, the nuns in this group were cared for by friends or married to suitors. All except Catharine von

Bora.

Catharine had been born in a little village twenty miles south of Leipzig in January 1499. Her mother's early death and her father's remarriage had placed her in a convent school at age five. She had received the veil at sixteen, when Luther was lecturing on Romans in Wittenberg. Two of her aunts were in the same convent.

In the general exodus from the monasteries, some of the young nuns at Nimbschen tried to escape. They were disciplined and guarded. Through a conspiracy with a businessman in Torgau, near Nimbschen, twelve of the nuns, including Catharine succeeded in making their escape on the night of April 4, 1523. They met in Catharine's rooms, escaped through the window to the garden, and then climbed the fence to the street. Hidden in empty beer barrels, they rode away from Nimbschen.

Catharine was twenty-four. Arriving in Wittenberg, she settled in the home of a wealthy citizen named Reichenbach, where for two years she helped with the housework. Toward the end of 1523 she fell in love with Jerome Baumgartner, a student guest in Melanchthon's home. They were engaged, and it seemed Catharine's future was secure.

But Baumgartner left Wittenberg and neglected Catharine, neither writing nor visiting. Luther interceded, writing to Baumgartner that he would like to see them married as soon as possible. Baumgartner refused his advice, announcing early the next year his engagement to the daughter of a wealthy family. Catharine understandably was quite hurt.

Not long afterward, a friend of Luther named Dr. Glatz courted Catharine and decided to marry her, but she refused and laughingly said she would marry only Dr. Amsdorf or Dr. Luther. The old companions who had journeyed together to Leipzig and Worms were coupled in warfare once again!

Luther suddenly decided to marry. For a long time his father had been urging him to. Hans, with his strong family feelings, wanted to see Martin established in his own home. Grandchildren would delight the old man.

Luther connected his marriage, as he did everything else, with the Gospel. He wrote to a friend that he would marry to "please his father, tease the pope, and spite the devil." This was worded in his normal semihumorous vein, but the justification nevertheless described his state of mind. He loved and honored his father, and marriage would please him. He held the pope as his mortal enemy, and it would further indicate the irreconcilable breach. The devil, he thought, was behind the celibacy law of the Catholic Church, hoping to trick innocent priests into mortal sin; thus marriage would defeat the devil.

So Luther did not marry for youthful, idealistic affection but for the heroic, mature consummation of the evangelical life he now professed. Catharine von Bora held for him no youthful charms; he was forty-two, she twenty-six. His mind and heart, exposed for years to public life, were somewhat toughened. The long years of monastic discipline had given him complete control over himself. This decision was a choice, not an emotion.

Catharine was of a good family. She was capable of the duties that would fall on the wife of Martin Luther. She was strong, rugged, healthy, with vitality and good humor. Luther had seen her many times in Wittenberg, and when he heard she had said she would marry no one but him or Amsdorf, it probably piqued his curiosity just enough to cause him to investigate.

In the spring, he spoke to her of his hopes. It was not easy. They both had known the monastic life. He knew what would be said of them. He reminded her that he was under the death sentence from the pope and emperor.

Luther appreciated her love for Baumgartner, but his heart was gentle and his honor unassailable. They were immediately in harmony, and when once the gentle words were said, the differences in age and temperament dissolved. Catharine held him in high respect. He was the "great doctor," but also her lover.

On the evening of June 13, 1525, they were married in Luther's home by John Bugenhagen, a faculty colleague. After the quiet wedding, Luther sent invitations for a public announcement and festivities. On June 27, Hans and Margaret Luther and many friends gathered in Wittenberg to celebrate the marriage.

They received a rich silver goblet from the university. Among their other presents were a barrel of Eimbeck beer, good wine, silver, and gold. Archbishop Albert of Mayence sent them twenty gulden in gold; Martin refused it, but Catharine kept it.

They went to live in the rooms Luther had occupied in the Black Cloister. Lucas Cranach came to visit them often, and for his wedding gift he painted their portraits.

Europe went into turmoil with the report of the wedding. The bitter, unscrupulous tongues of Luther's more violent Catholic opponents lashed at him. Rumor was spread that it was a marriage of necessity—but this was too much even for Erasmus, who came to Luther's defense.

Erasmus defended only the rumor of scandal. He thought the wedding itself was a tragedy—or, as he said, the Reformation "started out like a tragedy but ended as all comedies do in a wedding." Rome predicted the Antichrist would result from the union (popular tradition expected the Antichrist to be born from the marriage of a monk and a nun). Erasmus again silenced the enemy with the remark that if such were the case, the Antichrist had had plenty of opportunities before this.

With rumors unchecked and the sources of information so impartial, it was impossible for Luther's marriage to be represented properly throughout Europe. Many a sincere and sensitive Catholic mind Luther had won earlier now were lost by what appeared to be an improper relationship. People could not forget Martin and Catharine each had taken in youth what were supposed to be irrevocable vows. Many did not share the power of the evangelical faith which had been, for Martin and Catharine, sufficient to break obedience to the vows.

Luther married with a clear expectation of the difficulties to follow. He was not prepared for the strange, quiet happiness that slowly came into his life as their home settled into a normal routine. Catharine brought to him a strong and willing service, a loyal and sympathetic heart, and a keen and delightful sense of humor. She was increasingly a source of joy and peace to him for the rest of his life.

The highest tribute he ever paid her was when he spoke one day of St. Paul's Epistle to the Romans: "This is my Catharine von Bora." In the Epistle to the Romans, Luther's heart first had found its religious peace.

THE MILLS OF GOD
1526-1545

In 1526, Luther's life settled into three types of activity. First, he had to carry on the great battle with the papacy and the state. Simultaneously he must construct the Evangelical Church in all its branches. Third, his home began increasingly to call for his attention and strength.

In the first of these fields he was technically an outlaw and had to be constantly on the lookout not to step unwarily into traps set for his capture. The Edict of Worms was supposed to be in force. Under its provisions, any German citizen was obligated to deliver Luther alive or dead to the authorities. His friends were careful not to allow strangers around his home or the university, fearing an assassin deeply loyal to the ancient church would take his life. Luther was unable to appear in person at any of the great meetings held during the fifteen years after Worms to try to heal the schism. The chief leader of the reforming party was forced to remain in seclusion. Attempts at reconciliation must be carried on through his subordinates, chiefly Melanchthon and Bucer.

The emperor was still pressing for clarification of the Lutheran issue. The first important diet after Worms was held in the German town of Speyer in 1526. Charles V was unable to attend because of the constant turmoil in European politics. The diet met at Speyer under the presidency of Charles' brother Ferdinand.

After a long debate, the Catholic party, headed by Ferdinand, insisted on the execution of the Edict of Worms. The Protestant party, headed by the Saxon elector, steadfastly refused to carry it out. They agreed that "each state should so live as it hoped to answer for its conduct to God and the emperor."

This was a victory for the reforming units of the empire. They were permitted to return to their states and continue their evangelical work.

At home in Wittenberg, Martin anxiously watched the work of Katie. Watching her, he knew the beauty of the stirring life that had brought the Magnificat to Mary's lips. Hans Luther had looked on Margaret Ziegler the same way through the late summer of 1483. Katie sat by Martin's side through many hours of reading and study, asking questions whenever the opportunity arose. Early in June they knew the wait would be over soon. Great was the rejoicing when, on June 6, Martin saw his firstborn son.

Old Hans Luther in Mansfield was notified he had a grandson, a namesake. While he waited for news from the diet, Martin Luther heard through the once-quiet cloister the cries of his baby. Katie nursed little Hans and wondered how life would be for him.

Continuing trouble in the south kept Charles from protesting too strongly against the action of the diet. He felt compelled to invade Italy because of the closeness between Pope Clement VII, nephew of Leo X, and the French cause. It was a strange spectacle indeed when Charles V, standard bearer of the Catholic faith in the north, ordered his army to march on the holy city.

Leo X had died in December 1521, while Luther had been in the Wartburg. He had been succeeded by Adrian VI, who had been Charles' private chaplain. Adrian's election had been dictated by the emperor. But Adrian was not equal to the strain, and in less than a year the cardinals convened for another election. They had had enough of Adrian's reform policies and joyfully welcomed another Medici. Clement was shrewd, luxury loving and secular, as his uncle had been.

Charles' army was composed of both Spanish and German soldiers. Men who had hissed and cheered Luther at the diet of Worms now found themselves marching together under a German general to attack Rome.

Benvenuto Cellini was in Rome at the time, doing work for Clement VII. As the northern army approached, the papal party took refuge in the impregnable castle of St. Angelo. They were in such a hurry to enter the castle that Cellini carried the train of the pope's robes as they ran for the quickly closing doors. One cardinal, unable to enter at the doors, was hoisted through a window. The Germans and Spaniards took the city on May 6 and thoroughly sacked it. Inside the castle, Cellini cleverly picked the jewels and melted the gold from papal ornaments so Clement VII in dire necessity might be able to pay his ransom.

Luther was sorry to hear of the sack of Rome. He preached and taught daily, and his health began to show signs of weakening under the long strain. As early as 1521, in the Wartburg he had experienced severe digestive disturbances. Throughout the month of March 1523, he had been afflicted with constant nausea and vomiting. Nervous headaches began the same month, never to leave him for the rest of his life. On July 6, 1527, rising from the dinner table, he fainted before he could reach his room. For days he was seriously ill.

Before his recovery was complete, the plague came again to Wittenberg. With its arrival the university moved to Jena—but not Luther, who never fled the plague. Catharine was carrying their second child. Little Hans, now more than a year old, fell desperately ill and for eleven days could neither eat nor drink.

Martin, weak and exhausted, summoned the strength to bear the burdens of home and church. One of his closest friends, who had stayed with him during the exodus to Jena, lost his wife to the plague, and Luther feared for Catharine's life.

It was a time of deep misery and uncertainty. Death was all around him. The great authorities of his childhood, church and state, were battling each other. Yet Luther found strength through his faith in God. Poring over the Forty-Sixth Psalm, he knew the strength of the castle walls that crowned his Teutonic hills. He knew how, in the hour of battle, his people were safe behind these majestic fortresses. So he was safe in God, when death and destruction were all around him. He remembered how secure he had been from violence in the castle above Eisenach. The devil was behind these unhappy movements in the world, but God was his protection from the devil.

From this, his hour of deep distress, came his song of triumph:

> A mighty fortress is our God,
>> A bulwark never failing;
> Our helper he, amid the flood
>> Of mortal ills prevailing.
> For still our ancient foe

Doth seek to work us woe,
His craft and power are great;
And armed with cruel hate
On earth is not his equal.

And though this world with devils filled
    Should threaten to undo us;
We will not fear, for God hath willed
    His truth to triumph through us.
The prince of darkness grim,
We tremble not for him
His rage we can endure,
For lo, his doom is sure,
One little word shall fell him.

That word above all earthly powers,
    No thanks to them abideth;
The spirit and the gift are ours
    Through him who with us sideth.
Let goods and kindred go,
This mortal life also;
The body they may kill—
God's truth abideth still,
His kingdom is forever.

He also wrote the cadenced, solemn music for this, his marching song. While he hummed the melody into form, he watched Hans recover and rejoiced to see him strong again. Catharine weathered the plague and entered the last few weeks of her pregnancy in fair health.

A daughter was born December 10. They named the little girl Elizabeth. But she was not strong, and before a year had passed, they buried her.

Luther, writing to a friend just after Elizabeth's death, said, "Little Hans thanks you for the rattle of which he is inordinately proud. . . . My little daughter, Elizabeth, is dead. She has left me wonderfully sick at heart and almost womanish, I am so moved by pity for her. I could never have believed how a father's heart could soften for his child."

As though his work was not enough, he turned his attention to the condition of the parishes in the section of Germany that now was accepting reform. With Melanchthon and others, he journeyed through the Saxon province, visiting town after town, examining each one's educational system and church practices. This was tremendously hard work, with rough travel, uncomfortable lodging, and irregular food. But Luther felt keenly the tremendous need for education if his new church was to support itself.

On his return from the trip he called attention to the miserable state of instruction throughout the province. He insisted that pastors thoroughly reconstruct this phase of their work, and he set himself to writing a catechism. This work was completed two years after his journey through the province. In it is the full, accurate expression of Luther's entire belief.

The Smaller Catechism, which he designed for family and school use, set in gentle, quiet form all the familiar doctrines of historic Christianity. The Ten Commandments were to be memorized to create a sense of sin; the Apostle's Creed was to be memorized for the message of the great redemption from sin; and the Lord's Prayer was to be memorized for the constant spiritual sustenance it could bring to the believer.

When Luther handled this massive theology in catechetical form, his mind and heart sympathized with the little boys and girls who would have to learn it. His great gift for practical application was never put to better advantage than when he explained the doctrines of the church to little children.

Charles V, with his political troubles in Italy and France finally quieted, returned his attention to his rebellious Germany. In 1529 he called for a second diet to meet at Speyer. Controlling this diet in person, the emperor forced the delegates to annul the action of 1526. He succeeded in obtaining a majority vote to prohibit reformed worship.

In response, on April 19 the delegates from the Lutheran areas presented a formal protest to the diet. They stated that by the law of the empire, a majority decision of the present diet could not rescind the unanimous decision of the previous diet, and they would stand on the action of 1526. This protest was signed by the representatives of Saxony, Brandenburg, Brunswick, Hesse, Anhalt, and fourteen of the free cities.

From this point on, the party of non-Catholic adherents was called Protestant. Some of the signers of the protest were not supporters of Luther, so the term Protestant carried a broad connotation.

The emperor was unable to heal the breach, and the diet closed with the two parties well-defined. Receiving news of the diet at home in Wittenberg, Luther saw a political party grow out of his religious reform—and he was unable to control it.

His family life continued normally, despite political

tensions. On May 4, almost a year after her little sister had died, Magdalene Luther was born. She was named for Magdalene von Bora, Catharine's aunt, who had been a companion in the Nimbschen convent and who was now a well-loved member of the Wittenberg home.

The division in the Protestant party, obvious at Speyer, was caused by the rapid growth of a reforming movement in Switzerland headed by Ulrich Zwingli. Born at Wildhaus, Switzerland, in 1484, Zwingli was trained for the church and entered the ministry in 1506. His educational career had brought him close to the humanistic movement, and he thoroughly admired Erasmus. In his early days of preaching he was, as Luther, violently opposed to the abuses of popular Catholic life. His protests steadily grew into a reform movement in Zurich, where he was a pastor from 1519 until his death.

The center of the Zwinglian movement was intellectual and humane. Zwingli was not deeply concerned over the problem of sin—Luther's central issue. Zwingli spoke the language of the Christian humanist, Luther that of the old Catholic, and they could not understand each other. Zwingli had been living, in the accepted custom, with a common-law wife for several years before marriage of the clergy was incorporated into his reform movement. Keenly intelligent, deeply and broadly sympathetic, he was loved greatly by the people of Zurich and was utterly devoted to his pastoral service.

Those signing the protest at Speyer—who were more Zwinglian than Lutheran—desired greatly to unite the two forces of the reform movement. A leader able to press the issue was Philip of Hesse, then twenty-five years old. He was the strongest and most capable of the reform princes, and he urged a meeting between Zwingli and Luther.

When the invitation came to Luther at Wittenberg, he did not want to go. He distrusted the Zwinglians, coupling in his mind Zwingli with Carlstadt and Munzer. But for political reasons, the elector John bade him go. Philip arranged the meeting at his castle at Marburg.

Zwingli was overjoyed. He, too, was a man marked for destruction, traveling from Zurich at great personal risk. After a lovely visit at Strassburg, he started for Marburg with the Strassburg delegates. They arrived September 27, and were greeted graciously by Philip in person.

Journeying down from the north, a bit sullen, Luther reached Marburg on the thirtieth, accompanied by Melanchthon and Jonas. The men upon whom the union of Protestant forces depended were in conference for four days.

The meetings opened with Zwingli's gentle prayer: "Fill us, O Lord and Father of us all, we beseech Thee, with Thy gentle Spirit, and dispel on both sides all the clouds of misunderstanding and passion. Make an end to the strife of blind fury. Arise, O Christ, Thou Sun of Righteousness, and shine upon us. Alas! While we contend, we only too often forget to strive after holiness which Thou requirest from us all. Guard us against abusing our powers and enable us to employ them with all earnestness for the promotion of holiness. Amen."

Outside the actual meetings, the men enjoyed friendship and came to appreciate and admire each other. But in the conference sessions it was a different story. In the field of logic, the religious mind does not function easily. Zwingli was brilliant, clear, concise. He attacked the orthodox position of Luther on the Lord's Supper with all the arguments of the humanists. But Luther was adamant.

They had known from the beginning that the major controversy would be over the presence of the body of Christ in the Communion. On this point Luther defended the doctrine of the Real Presence.

They were seated at a wooden table, Luther and Melanchthon on one side, Zwingli and Oecolampadius opposite. The argument was linked necessarily to scriptural texts; Luther said he would not be convinced in this matter by any other authority.

In the first severe clash of opinion, Luther took a piece of chalk and wrote on the table, "Hoc est corpus Meum." In every crisis thereafter he pointed to the text and said it stood unanswered.

Oecolampadius quoted John 6:63: "It is the spirit that quickeneth; the flesh profiteth nothing."

Zwingli tried to press this advantage too far, saying to Luther, "That passage breaks your neck." This was a Swiss idiom for a conclusive refutation, but Luther didn't receive it as such and was angered. He held that John 6:63 had no connection with the institution of the Last Supper. The Landgrave Philip's interference happily saved the conference.

Many times they came to harsh words. At the end, though unable to agree, they offered mutual apologies for the outbursts. The emotional Zwingli declared he wanted the friendship of the Wittenbergers above all men on earth.

Philip asked them to draw up a statement of belief that all could sign. Luther wrote out a definition of fifteen cardinal doctrines, showing their agreement in all but the last, which concerned the Lord's Supper. The delegates signed the document.

Zwingli offered his hand to Luther, saying that despite their disagreement they could remain brothers. But Luther made a clear distinction between brotherhood and friendship. Brotherhood to him involved a common belief and common communion; with Zwingli denying the essential doctrine of Luther's heart, there could be no brotherhood. He refused the offered hand. After the sessions closed, however, they parted with hearty handshakes of personal friendship.

As Luther traveled northward, he was conscious of the fact that Melanchthon had been particularly silent throughout the meeting at Marburg. He sensed Philip was more Catholic than he and much farther removed from Zwingli.

The Lutheran and Swiss reforms thereafter went their separate ways. Zwingli returned to Zurich to continue his plans for organizing a political Protestant party around the northern Swiss states, with the cooperation of Philip of Hesse. He died heroically four years later when Switzerland was torn by religious civil war. Marching as chaplain with the troops of Zurich, he was killed at the second battle of Cappel.

The best effort Charles V made to reconcile the differences in Germany was at Augsburg in 1530. Thomas Lindsay in his *History of the Reformation* described Charles' entrance into Augsburg:

> The summons to the Diet, commanding the
> Electors, princes, and all the Estates of the

Empire to meet at Augsburg on the 8th of
April, 1530, had been issued when Charles
was at Bologna. No threats marred the invitation. The Emperor announced that he meant
to leave all past errors to the judgment of the
Saviour; that he wished to give a charitable
hearing to every man's opinions, thoughts,
and ideas; and that his only desire was to
secure that all might live under the one
Christ, in one Commonwealth, one Church,
and one Unity. He left Innsbruck on the 6th
of June, and, traveling slowly, reached the
bridge on the Lech, a little distance from
Augsburg, on the evening of the 15th. There
he found the great princes of the Empire who
had been waiting his arrival from two o'clock
in the afternoon. They alighted to do him
reverence, and he graciously dismounted also,
and greeted them with all courtesy. Charles
had brought the papal nuncio, Cardinal
Campeggio, in his train. Most of the Electors
knelt to receive the Cardinal's blessing; but
John of Saxony stood bolt upright and refused
the proffered benediction.

The procession—one of the most gorgeous
Germany had ever seen—was marshaled for
the ceremonial entry into the town. The
retinues of the Electors were all in their ap-
propriate colors and arms—Saxony, by ancient prescriptive right, leading the van. Then
came the Emperor alone, a baldachino carried
over his head. He had wished the nuncio and

his brother to ride beside him under the
canopy; but the Germans would not suffer it;
no Pope's representative was to be permitted
to ride shoulder to shoulder with the head of
the German Empire entering the most important of his imperial cities.

At the gates of the town, the clergy, singing
the "Advenisti desiderabilis," met the procession. All—Emperor, clergy, princes, and their
retinues—entered the cathedral. The Te
Deum was sung, and the Emperor received
the benediction. Then the procession reformed, and accompanied Charles to his
lodgings in the Bishop's Palace.

In response to this summons the Saxon elector, in
company with Luther and Melanchthon, had waited at
Coburg, the southernmost town in the province, for
word of safe conduct from the emperor. When it arrived,
it omitted Luther's name. While the elector, Melanchthon,
and the rest of the company journeyed on to Augsburg,
Luther took refuge in the great castle overlooking the
town of Coburg. He remained there from April 25
through October 4.

These were bitter days for him. He was sick and
discouraged, but he kept himself busy. He finished the
translation of Jeremiah, began Ezekiel, and completed all
the lesser prophets. He published some of Æsop's fables
in German and wrote 12 other complete works. There
are 123 letters preserved from these months in the
Coburg castle.

All the while, he received messages from Augsburg,

where the diet was in session. They told how the evangelical princes refused to march in the Corpus Christi procession through the streets of Augsburg. They told how stalwart George of Brandenburg had told the emperor—whom he loved—that rather than deny his God he would kneel then and allow his head to be cut off. They told how steadfastly his friends were maintaining the faith.

But Luther grew anxious when they brought him news that Melanchthon was drawing up the great confession. Melanchthon was a bit too conciliatory for Luther, who always feared the younger man would concede too much to the papists. The fear was well-grounded, for Melanchthon was eager, above all else, to heal the break.

Terrific loyalties conflicted in Melanchthon's mind. The nephew of Reuchlin could not understand the necessity of the departure; the friend of Erasmus still honored the mother church. But these loyalties were overpowered by his tremendous affection for and belief in Martin Luther.

Now, in Augsburg, he did his best to phrase a conciliatory statement. The confession of the Protestant princes written by Melanchthon was read in the diet on July 25 by Christian Bayer, chancellor of Saxony.

It was a clear, concise statement containing two sections. In the first it set forth the religious views of the Lutherans. In the second it listed the abuses which must be corrected. It was theologically conservative. Luther rejoiced when word came that they had been permitted to read their confession before the Diet, but his rejoicing was short-lived, for Charles asked a group of papal theologians, headed by Eck of Ingolstadt, to prepare an answer.

Here is seen once again the deadly fault in the imperial policy. Eck was a bitter man. Five times his report was returned to the committee for softening and revision. When it finally was brought forth, it still was too harsh for the Lutherans.

John, the elector of Saxony, called "the Steadfast" by his people, refused to remain at the diet under such conditions and departed after a difficult scene with the emperor. Charles V and John admired each other, and the elector honored his emperor with the ancient civil loyalty of the Germans. But this was a case where his emperor required the surrender of his conscience. He told Charles he must stand by his faith.

Charles' final words to him were: "Uncle, uncle, I did not expect this from you." Tears were in the elector's eyes as he turned his back on his sovereign and started northward.

Meanwhile, Luther waited anxiously. During a week of sickness a messenger arrived from Wittenberg bringing little gifts from Catharine and the family, including a picture painted by Lucas Cranach of the one-year-old Magdalene. Luther held it lovingly in his hands and remarked to his secretary, "She is so dark. She does not look like Magdalene. She has the mouth of Hans." He hung it on the wall in his study, where it was a constant source of joy.

Luther was unhappy, separated from his family, and he corresponded faithfully. His son Hans was now four. Luther remembered the laughing, playing boy. He wrote him:

(Feste Coburg, June 19, 1530)

Grace and peace in Christ, dear little son. I am glad to hear that you are studying and saying your prayers. Continue to do so, my son, and when I come home I will bring you a pretty present.

I know a lovely, pleasant garden where many children are; they wear golden jackets and gather nice apples under the trees and pears and cherries and purple plums, and sing and run and jump and are happy and have pretty little ponies with golden reins and silver saddles. I asked the man who owned the garden whose children they were. He said: "They are the children who say their prayers and study and are good." Then said I: "Dear man, I also have a son whose name is Hans Luther; may he come into the garden and eat the sweet apples and pears and ride a fine pony and play with these children?" Then said the man: "If he says his prayers and is good, he can come into the garden, and Phil and Justy, too, and when they all come they shall have whistles and drums and fifes and dance and shoot little cross-bows." Then he showed me a fine large lawn in the garden for dancing, where hang real golden whistles and fine silver cross-bows. But it was yet too early and the children had not finished eating and I could not wait to see them dance, so I said to the man: "My dear sir, I must go away and write at once to my dear little Hans about all this, so that he will say his prayers and study and be good, so that he may come into the

garden, and he has an Auntie Lena whom he
must bring with him." Then the man said: "All
right, go and tell him about it." So, dear little
Hans, study and say your prayers and tell Phil
and Justy to say their prayers and study, too, so
you may all come into the garden together. God
bless you. Give Auntie Lena my love and a kiss
from me.

> *Your loving father,*
> *Martin Luther*

While his heart was entranced and his mind happy with meditations on the life of little Hans, John Reinicke, the friend of his school days, brought him news that old Hans was dead. Luther had left Wittenberg for Coburg knowing of his father's sickness. He had written that he was unable to come to Mansfield and had gently recalled to Hans, in his last letter, the faith in which they lived. The pastor at Mansfield read the letter to Hans and asked if he believed this faith. Hans replied, "Aye, he would be a knave who didn't."

It had been thirty-three years since the two boys, John and Martin, had left their homes in Mansfield for school in Magdeburg. Luther could picture Hans now as he had been in those days long past. He heard, as if in a dream, Reinicke telling him how old Hans had died.

Gone. Life over. His father's spirit at the last great judgment.

Luther rose, took his psalter and entered the study, where he stayed for almost two days in unnerved sorrowing. Forty-seven years before Hans had carried his little boy to Bartholomew Rennebecher for baptism, and now the little boy's heart, welded to his father through years of affection, was broken.

But prayer and faith again were his sources of strength. Near the close of the second day he regained control and picked up the routine of life.

A few days later his friend Wenzel Link opened a letter from Luther and read:

> *Now I am sorrowful, for I have received tidings of the death of my father, that dear and gentle old man whose name I bear, and although I am glad for his sake that his journey to Christ was so easy and pious and that, freed from the monsters of this world, he rests in peace, nevertheless my heart is moved to sorrow. For under God, I owe my life and bringing up to him.*

The Diet of Augsburg closed unhappily for the Protestants. Luther returned to Wittenberg in the fall knowing that imperial pressure would be more severe than ever. From now on it would be a battle of political alliances, with Luther more and more in the background. He watched through the succeeding years the organization of the Schmaldkalden League for the protection of the reformed territory, with Hesse and Saxony at its head. He heard of the riotings in Munster and the murderous overthrow of the Anabaptists gathered there. With the death of Clement VII and the election of Paul III, he knew the Catholic Church now was controlled by a strong and able pope. He watched with interest the long game of political chess between Henry VIII and the papacy, climaxing in the severance of England's loyalty to Rome.

In 1539 he read a book by the young John Calvin and wrote him a letter of commendation, but he did not sense that under Calvin's control the Swiss city of Geneva would rise to a prominence equal that of Wittenberg. He heard of the formation of the Society of Jesus, but he did not know that behind the society was a spirit as intense and devoted as his own, and superior in organizational ability. He was relieved to learn of the defeat and retreat of the Turks from Vienna; he trembled, with the rest of Europe, at the narrow escape from control by Suliman the Magnificent. He mourned the death of the Elector John but rejoiced that his successor, John Frederick, was a staunch Protestant.

Throughout this troubled time, he was seldom called into actual leadership. He journeyed in 1537 to Schmaldkalden, where he struggled to draw up a confession of faith emphasizing the differences between Protestants and Catholics more strongly than the "Augsburg Confession." Many other Protestant leaders were there, as was the papal nuncio, Vergerio, trying to institute conciliatory proceedings. Luther's health broke; he suffered the severely painful affliction known as "the stone." He longed again for his wife and children, fearing he would never see them again.

John Frederick ordered him carried home, and sent word ahead for Catharine von Bora to meet him on the way. Luther traveled in John Frederick's own carriage; the jolting caused such agony they could take him only two miles the first day.

Relief came during the night. The messenger who rode back to Schmaldkalden with news of Luther's recovery was so happy he stopped by the papal legate's window and shouted "Luther lives!" before he took the word to John Frederick.

Though returned to health, Luther felt rather uncertain of life. On the way home, at Gotha, he wrote his first will, beginning: "God be praised, I know I did right to attack the papacy which injures the cause of God, Christ, and the Gospel!" It closed: "Now I commend my soul into the hands of my Lord Jesus Christ whom I have preached and confessed on earth."

He returned to Wittenberg to continue his labors, but life was increasingly painful. The severity of his headaches, severe rheumatism, the recurring digestive disturbances, neuritis in his chest, and a dizzying disease in the middle ear all plagued him.

In 1539 Duke George of Saxony, the fairest and staunchest Catholic defender, died. His successor was an admirer of Luther and an adherent to the reformed faith. Luther rode from Wittenberg to Leipzig to attend the installation. Once again he stood in the hall of the ducal palace where, twenty years before, he had debated with John Eck. He had a deep, quiet sense of victory now as he stood to proclaim, in this room, the evangelical faith. His appearance at Leipzig in 1519 had been the prelude to a long, stern warfare. The warfare was not over, but already he could see lasting consequences, and he was glad to add Leipzig to his inheritance.

The rejoicing quickly turned to trouble. Philip of Hesse came to Luther for advice regarding his unhappy marriage. At nineteen, Philip had married the daughter of Duke George. They had never been happy. They repelled each other and had not lived together for years. At first, Philip had taken the conventional escape from his misery by keeping a mistress. But he was affected by the reforming work of Luther and Zwingli, and his conscience troubled him greatly. Having long since dismissed his mistress, he recently had fallen in love with a young lady of the Leipzig court. Her mother refused to let them marry unless Philip either was divorced or obtained permission from the great Protestant preachers for this second marriage without dissolving the first.

Luther talked it over with Melanchthon and Bucer. The Wittenberg theologians went to Eisenach and met Philip's representatives. Philip presented his case clearly and decisively. But he had not told Luther of his mistress; Luther thought his case was more honorable than it really was.

The question of a man having two wives was open, in European thought. Cardinal Campeggio had actually suggested it to Clement VII in discussing Henry VIII's request. Luther firmly believed the church had the right to authorize it in special cases for the protection of morals and character. This was a practice of the ancient church. Luther believed that as Protestant pastors they had the right to depart from the normal moral law. The church often had argued that when a man's wife was stricken with leprosy or insanity it was quite within the realm of moral law that, without deserting her, he could marry a second wife.

In handing down their decision in Philip's case, Luther, Melanchthon, and Bucer quoted the Old Testament. They argued they were no better than Abraham, Isaac, and other patriarchs who had enjoyed this privilege. They then affirmed that there was no prohibition of bigamy in the New Testament. It was commonly accepted Christian law that a man should have but one wife, they knew, but here was a special case.

All parties to the agreement were willing. They granted Philip of Hesse permission to marry.

They did this under what they called the seal of the confessional, requiring secrecy from all parties. If the agreement became public information, the marriage would be dissolved and revert to concubinage.

This was their fatal error. It was impossible to keep this secret. Within months, Luther once again was the center of a storm of protest. He had sanctioned the breaking of a moral law, defying the accepted canons of Christianity.

He accepted this attack as he accepted all abuse, defending his course with the open honesty he had always shown. But the damage was irreparable. Philip was hurt deeply by the criticism heaped on him by other Protestant princes, and his fine leadership was no longer available for Lutheranism.

Meanwhile, the inner life of the Lutheran Church developed steadily. A man of deep historic piety, Luther constantly struggled to impart this feeling to his people. The translation of the Bible, begun at the Wartburg and continuing through the disastrous days of 1530, finally was completed in 1534. The last edition to have his personal supervision came in 1545.

In his translation work, Luther struggled to create a version understandable by all Germans. He succeeded far beyond his fondest dreams. So powerful was his work that it practically created a new German language. Since the Bible was being read feverishly by hundreds of thousands of Germans, the imprint of Luther's style and phrasing was permanent.

He also brought into the German language the great Catholic services in which he had been raised. The Mass, the central point in Lutheran worship, was set in German under Luther's personal editorship. He produced a series of noble hymns for public worship.

During the bitter days after the Diet at Worms, prosecution of the edict, in July 1523, had raised the first Lutheran martyrs in the Netherlands. Luther was tremendously disturbed to hear that two young men, affirming their confidence in the new faith, had been put to death. He would have stood in their places. Unable to do so, he celebrated their confession by writing his first hymn, a powerful, militant appeal beginning "Ein neues Lied wir heben an."* They were indeed uplifting a new song. Steadily, Luther added hymn after hymn to his church's worship. They were bold, martial, triumphant expressions, addressing the doctrine of redemption and revolving around the blood and sacrifice of Jesus. Immersed in the ancient psalms and their adaptation in Catholic hymnody, he brought these, too, to the German tongue. The One Hundred Thirtieth Psalm became "Aus tiefer Not schrei ich zu dir," the twelfth "Ach Gott, vom Himmel sieh darein." The Lutherans sang "Te Deum laudamus" as "Herr Gott, dich loben wir." The "Veni Creator Spiritus" uplifted them in "Kom, Gott, Schöpfer, heiliger Geist."

He sensitively furnished both music and words for the rhythm of his movement. Loveliest of all his hymns, perhaps, are those he wrote for his children. Many were the evenings in the Luther home when father, mother,

---

*German for "a new song we sing"

and children sang their Christian faith. Luther appreciated the gentleness, beauty, and simplicity of a child's understanding. When the family entered the Christmas season together, he told the story of Bethlehem so his sons and daughters could understand it. For them he wrote *"Von Himmel kam der Engel Schaar, Vom Himmel hoch da komin ich her"** and our familiar "Away in a Manger, No Crib for His Bed." The student who had sung lustily in the streets of Magdeburg and Eisenach now sang from new experiences the gentle songs of Christian childhood. He who had carried his lute on the all-important journey to the Imperial Diet, singing and playing in the evenings as he rested at the inns along the way, now applied to music the joyous, triumphant strain of his Christian life.

Many a heart unable to fathom the depths of Melanchthon's theology found rich comfort in the songs from Luther's soul. Year after year as he grew older, he could hear his German people marching victoriously to the rhythm of his music. His religious life expressed itself between the cradle songs of Jesus and the strong fortress of God.

Katie von Bora had plenty to do during these hectic years. Managing a household with insufficient finances is hard enough, but she had many other tasks. Luther's salary did not cover his needs, even though he received many presents, including a pension from the king of Denmark for services rendered to the church. There were always friends and guests to be given lodging and food. Over the years eleven orphaned relatives found

---

*German for "The Angels came from heaven, from heaven I come from"

support in Luther's home.

Two of the orphan nephews, George Kaufmaun and Hans Polnerd caused trouble. They took great liberty with the house and town, drinking and carousing. The finger of gossip and scorn was pointed at their great uncle. Attempting to control them, Luther pointed out how his every action was reported throughout the world, and how they were bringing disgrace on the reform cause as well as on himself.

He told Hans Polnerd one day, "Other men when drunk are happy and mild, as my father was. They sing and joke, but you fall into a fury. Such men ought to flee drink like a poison, for it is a deadly poison to such natures. . ."

Luther was thoroughly unsystematic in the use of money. He never sold a book or manuscript in his life, steadfastly refusing, although printers offered him hundreds of dollars a year for his written works. These, he said, were the gifts of God and were not for sale. Nor did he receive a salary for teaching. He was supported after the break from the monastic order by an annual gift from the elector, which was increased steadily until it reached 400 gulden. But even with this he wrote a pathetic letter one day to a friend who had asked him for money, saying there was no money to be had—they even were pawning their wedding gifts.

Lucas Cranach, ever a friend in need, loaned him money steadily. The family had cattle, a large garden, and a fish pond to support themselves. They owned a farm a few miles from Wittenberg on the road to Zulsdorf, which Katie managed.

They had no privacy. Luther's tremendous reputation and the insatiable curiosity of his followers kept the family constantly in the public eye.

But underneath the stress of this visible life was a very quiet, gentle current. Katie and Martin loved each other more dearly as the years passed. Their conversation around the home and their correspondence reveals a steady banter that revealed a very happy affection. She never lost her high respect for him—but neither did she surrender her independent will. Luther often laughingly told Melanchthon and other friends that he had merely exchanged one authority for another when he married. Katie expressed her opinions, even with guests present. Luther called these expressions "sermons." He often told her he wished she would preface the sermon with a prayer; he knew she would pray so long she would never get to the sermon!

Luther was particularly happy with the smallest children in the house. He constantly held his youngest child in his lap, talking and playing. Having lost one daughter in infancy, Luther watched the growth of his second daughter, Magdalene, with tender, sensitive affection. He knew the heights of a father's love as she grew nearer and dearer to him. When Magdalene became seriously ill in September 1542, he entered the depths of human sorrow. One who was with him through this trial wrote:

> As his daughter lay very ill, Dr. Luther said:
> "I love her very much, but, dear God, if it be
> thy will to take her, I submit to thee." Then
> he said to her as she lay in bed: "Magdalene,
> my dear little daughter, would you like to stay
> here with your father, or would you willingly
> go to your Father yonder?" She answered:

"Darling father, as God wills." Then said he: "Dearest child, the spirit is willing but the flesh is weak." Then he turned away and said: "I love her very much; if my flesh is so strong, what can my spirit do? God has given no bishop so great a gift in a thousand years as he has given me in her. I am angry with myself that I cannot rejoice in heart and be thoughtful as I ought."

Now as Magdalene lay in the agony of death, her father fell down before the bed on his knees and wept bitterly and prayed that God might free her. Then she departed and fell asleep in her father's arms.

As they laid her in the coffin he said: "Darling Lena, you will rise and shine like a star, yea, like the sun. . . . I am happy in spirit, but the flesh is sorrowful and will not be content; the parting grieves me beyond measure. . . . I have sent a saint to heaven."

Justus Jonas, always close to Luther's mind when big events occurred, received the following letter from Luther a few days after Magdalene died:

> *I believe that you have already heard that my dearest daughter Magdalene has been reborn to the eternal kingdom of Christ; and although my wife and I ought to give thanks and rejoice at such a happy pilgrimage and blessed end, whereby she has escaped the power of the flesh, the world, the Turk, and the devil, yet so strong*

> *is natural affection that we must sob and groan
> in heart under the oppression of killing grief. . . .
> Would that I and all mine might have such a
> death, or rather such a life. She was, as you
> know, of a sweet, gentle, and loving nature.*

The constant pressure of twenty-five years of public life was breaking Luther. He grew touchy and sensitive. He felt Wittenberg no longer honored him properly and no one paid any attention to him. The stern ethics he preached were disregarded by the villagers.

In the late spring of 1545 he traveled to the town of Zeitz, south of Leipzig. His son Hans was with him. Luther decided to stay away forever from the town he thought was repudiating his leadership. He sent this letter to his wife:

> *Dear Katie:*
> *. . . . I should like to arrange not to go back to
> Wittenberg. My heart has grown cold so that I do
> not care to live there, but wish you would sell the
> garden and the farm, house and buildings, except
> the big house, which I should like to give back to
> my gracious lord. Your best course would be to
> go to Zulsdorf; while I am alive you could im-
> prove the little estate with my salary, for I hope
> my gracious lord will let my salary go on at least
> during this last year of my life. After my death
> the four elements will not suffer you to live at
> Wittenberg, therefore it will be better for you to
> do during my lifetime what you will have to do
> after my death. It looks as if Wittenberg and her*

*government would catch—not St. Vitus' dance or
St. John's dance, but the beggars' dance and
Beelzebub's dance; the women and girls have
begun to go bare before and behind and there is
no one to punish or correct them and God's word
is mocked. Away with this Sodom. . . . Day after
tomorrow I am going to Merseburg, for Prince
George has pressed me to do so. I will wander
around here and eat the bread of charity before I
will martyr and soil my poor old last days with
the disordered life of Wittenberg, where I lose all
my bitter, costly work. You may tell Melanchthon
and Bugenhagen this, if you will, and ask the
latter to give Wittenberg my blessing, for I can no
longer bear its wrath and displeasure. God bless
you. Amen.*

Martin Luther

Wittenberg was not to let such a tragedy occur and sent Melanchthon, Bugenhagen, the burgomaster, and the elector's physician to bring Luther home. They met him in Merseburg, paid him due honor, and brought him home in triumph.

The evening of life had come.

seven

Winter

DEAR GENESIS
1545-1546

O<small>N</small> N<small>OVEMBER</small> 10, 1545, there was a birthday celebration in the Luther home. Old friends came to honor the man they loved.

Katie, as ever, was efficient and thoughtful. Hans, home from school, was now nineteen. Martin was fourteen, Paul twelve, and Margaret ten. Song and laughter rang through the rooms.

But Luther's heart did not rejoice. The infirmities of age weighed heavily on him. Like a stranger in a foreign land, he longed for the sweetness of death. He wanted peace and quiet, but the world would not permit it. Now, certain of approaching death, he lived in two worlds. In the present world he loved and enjoyed Katie, children, and friends. But in the world of the spirit he could almost commune with his Lord and Master. He felt a strong sense of companionship with the dead—with his father Hans and mother Margaret, Elizabeth, and Magdalene.

He looked at Katie across the room filled with friends. She was older and stouter now. Time had taken a heavy toll from her. He thought of the iron will that had carried her and her family through many hard hours. He saw her hands, roughened by the work of house and farm. In his heart he thanked God for her life and love.

Her eye caught his, and quickly she was at his side to touch his hand and ask his slightest wish. Friends departed and night settled over them.

It had been sixty-two years since the sun had gone down on his parents with their new child. Sixty-two years! He had been an instrument in the hands of God, he believed. He had followed his conscience through all circumstances. His mind had been set staunchly in the written word of God, but his conscience rather than the Word had been his guide.

God had been merciful. Tomorrow he would finish his present lecture series and then be through. Tired and anxious for his homegoing, he slept.

The next day he lectured on the book of Genesis. He closed his notebook, looked up gently, and quietly told his students, "This is dear Genesis. God grant that others do better with it after me. I am weak. Pray God to grant me a good, blessed hour."

He left the lecture hall around which, for one mighty hour, he had held the swinging, whirling universe. Dear Genesis! Yes, dear indeed. In the beginning God created. . . . Let there be light. . . . and . . . it was good . . . male and female created he them . . . the serpent . . . the seed of the woman . . . in the sweat of thy brow . . . in travail!

His race was not yet run. In his childhood home of Mansfield, Counts Albert and Gebhardt were in bitter dispute, and only Luther could solve the difficulty. He left for Mansfield in a cold December storm. He spent Christmas there, but his heart was in Wittenberg with

Katie. Then Melanchthon's health broke, and Luther returned home in January with the dispute unsettled.

On January 23 he left home again. Katie begged him not to go because of his health and the bitter weather. But Luther had known only duty for too long. He could not spare himself. In tears wrung from honest love and a presentiment of death, he kissed his "Lord Katie" goodbye.

His sons Hans, Martin, and Paul went with him, as did his friend John Aurifaber. Two days' journey brought them to Halle, where they were delayed by a flooding of the Saale River. He wrote lovingly to Katie, joking that a lady of the Anabaptist persuasion detained them.

Crossing the flood, they reached Eisleben, where he wrote home describing the journey:

I wish you grace and peace in Christ, and send you my poor, old, infirm love. Dear Katie, I was weak on the road to Eisleben, but that was my own fault. . . . As I drove through the village such a cold wind blew from behind through my cap on my head that it was like to turn my brain to ice. This may have helped my vertigo, but now, thank God, I am so well that I am sore tempted by fair women and care not how gallant I am . . . .

Your little sons went to Mansfield day before yesterday, after they had humbly begged Jack-an-apes to take them. I don't know what they are doing; if it were cold they might freeze, but as it is warm they may do or suffer what they like. God bless you with all my household and remem-

ber me to my table companions.

> *Your old lover,*
> *M.L.*

The negotiations continued in Eisleben. Luther hoped to solve the problem through brotherly love and affection, but the lawyers, he said, made it difficult.

His boys were with relatives in Mansfield. His mind was in Wittenberg. On February 14 he wrote again:

> *Grace and peace in the Lord. Dear Katie, we hope to come home this week if God wills. God has shown great grace to the lords, who have been reconciled in all but two or three points. It still remains to make the brothers Count Albert and Count Gebhardt real brothers; this I shall undertake today and shall invite both to visit me, that they may see each other, for hitherto they have not spoken, but have embittered each other by writing. But the young lords and the young ladies, too, are happy and make parties for fools' bells and skating, and have masquerades, and are all very jolly, even Count Gebhardt's son. So we see that God hears prayers.*
>
> *I send you the trout given me by the Countess Albert. She is heartily happy at this union.*
>
> *Your little sons are still at Mansfield. James Luther will take care of them. We eat and drink like lords here and they wait on us so well—too well, indeed, for they might make us forget you at Wittenberg. Moreover I am no more troubled*

with the stone. Jonas' leg has become right bad; it is looser on the shin-bone, but God will help it.

You may tell Melanchthon and Bugenhagen and Cruciger everything.

A report has reached here that Dr. Martin Luther has left for Leipzig or Magdeburg. Such tales are invented by those silly wiseacres, your countrymen. Some say the Emperor is thirty miles from here, at Soest in Westphalia; some say that the French and the Landgrave of Hesse are raising troops. Let them say and sing; we will wait on God. God bless you.

Dr. Martin Luther

Three days later the counts signed an agreement settling the dispute. Luther's work was done. The boys came from Mansfield, and preparations for the homeward journey were made.

But Luther was sick. Faint would not leave so easily now. He felt a tightness in the chest. Hot towels and brandy helped, and he tried to sleep. But the ailment kept its grip on him. He could not rest quietly. At two o'clock in the morning of the eighteenth, he roused his friends and lay down on a couch. Jonas, ever faithful, was there. Colius, the Mansfield preacher, had come down. One of the countesses of Mansfield, also staying at the inn, came to the room. Martin and Paul stood by their father's side.

The agony increased. Terrific pain seized him—but he was accustomed to pain. He called on Jonas and Colius to pray for the great battle within the church. Then phrases of Scripture were heard from his lips. Three

197

times he repeated, "God so loved the world, that he gave his only begotten Son, that whosoever believeth in him should not perish, but have everlasting life." His boys heard him whisper, "Father, into Thy hands I commend my spirit."

The pain would not subside. Jonas asked, "Dear Father, will you stand by Christ and the doctrine you have preached?"

Stand by Christ and the doctrine? In the hour of death? Luther's mighty will held off the coming stroke, and he answered, "Yes."

In the final moment, his halting voice whispered the glorious message, "Who . . . hath . . . my word . . . shall . . . not . . . see . . . death. . . ."

Then darkness.

His body was taken back over the beloved road to Wittenberg. On February 22 they buried him in the cathedral church. Melanchthon preached.

Katie gathered her children around her that night in the Black Cloister. Later, she wrote to Christina von Bora:

Wittenberg, April 2, 1546

Grace and peace in God the Father of our Lord Jesus Christ. Kind, dear sister! I can easily believe that you have hearty sympathy with me and my poor children. Who would not be sorrowful and mourn for so noble a man as was my dear lord, who much served not only one city, or a single land, but the whole world? Truly, I am so distressed that I cannot tell my great heart sorrow to anyone, and neither can I sleep. If I had

had a principality, or an empire, it would never have cost me so much pain to lose them as I have now that our Lord God has taken from me, and not from me only, but from the whole world, this dear and precious man. . . .

eight

Spring Comes Again

THE LIVING SPIRIT
1546-1933

THE WORLD WOULD not let Luther rest. He had set a mighty force in motion, and long before his physical death, that power had transcended his limitations to make its way in the land.

Charles V continued to strive to bring his domains under control. At the head of a victorious army he entered Wittenberg in 1547, one year after Luther's death. Catharine, fleeing the emperor's approach, was thrown from her cart on the rough roads. She never recovered from her injuries and shock.

In the castle church, Charles stood before Luther's grave. It had been twenty-six years since they had seen each other at Worms. Then, Charles had not been much impressed by the strong, intense Augustinian—but now half his empire was enthralled by the monk's high ideal! Medieval practice tempted Charles to dig up and scatter the heretic's dust, as Wyclif's ashes had been scattered. But Charles placed honor above such an action. He is reported to have said, "I make war on the living, not on the dead."

Luther's spirit was living indeed, and the warfare continued. Men with Luther's vision carried on the battle for freedom. Luther had risen to protest abuse within a system. The defenders, refusing to consider correction, had brought the attack directly against the system itself. Luther understood the abuse to be within the Roman— not the Catholic—aspect of the system. But many had been too long accustomed to Roman authority to follow the new leadership easily.

The rising tide of nationalism was ready for Luther's attack on Rome's power. Yet Luther was not really a nationalist. He would rather have surrendered all of Germany than seen the creation of a German church that was not Catholic and Christian, with an evangelical emphasis. The nationalistic backing furnished Luther with necessary temporal support in his revolt from Rome, but it was in no way integral to the religious issue. A state church—with the implication that the state dictates the thought of corporate or individual Christians— was unthinkable in Luther's doctrine. He would have opposed Hitler as decisively as he would have Lenin.

The differences between the Roman and Lutheran concepts of Catholicism were disputed in political warfare. The battle raged over central Europe for all too long. The pure religious issue was lost early. The long struggle became a confusion of dynastic, national, economic, and religious issues.

A pitiful attempt at peace in Augsburg in 1555 brought only a breathing period. The warring parties agreed that the prince of any given political unit should decide the form of religion his subjects should adopt. If they disapproved the prince's choice, the subjects could move to another province. This freedom to move was an advance over the Roman Catholic policy, where one could move only to the next world—via the stake—if he or she disagreed with Roman dogma.

Events came swiftly following the break-up of the medieval world. Luther could claim for his own Scotland, Denmark, Scandinavia, northern Germany, northern Switzerland, the Protestant units in France and the Netherlands (Huguenots), and smaller groups in England. England proper was not his.

Ulrich Zwingli's followers in Switzerland sustained their independence from Wittenberg in thought and practice, but not their freedom from Rome. That victory was Luther's alone.

John Calvin, the leader in France, moved into the evangelical faith under direct Lutheran influence while being taught New Testament Greek by a German of Wittenberg sympathies. Calvin then combined his gifts of clarity, precision, indomitable will, and rich humility with the Lutherans' scriptural authority to construct the powerful Puritan theology.

At the feet of Calvin, the Scottish leader John Knox learned the inner strength of the independent evangelical faith. In Edinburgh he built the foundations of the stern and lovely piety of the Presbyterians.

But all these movements, as well as Lutheranism, soon moved far from the basic strength of Martin Luther. They defined faith and doctrinal standards so strictly that the ancient freedom of Christians again was denied.

Through the years, the spirit of the great Saxon has touched his people. Pietist and Moravian both have held it for a moment. In England, when the common people heard the evangelical message preached by the Wesleys and Whitefield, it was the voice of Luther. His commentaries on Romans and Galatians were the cradles of the Wesleyan life.

And what of his great enemy? The Roman church, whose historic Catholicism was the center and soul of Luther's life, should number him among the saints. In an hour when everything Catholicism holds dear was disappearing from the church's leadership, he stood valiantly for Catholic tradition. Julius II, Leo X, and Clement VII had brought to the verge of ruin the authority of the church in thought and practice. Cardinal Cajetan at Augsburg, John Eck at Leipzig, the cardinal archbishop of Mayence, Aleander at Worms—all were willing to sacrifice God and the human soul to Roman power. Luther fought, against his Catholic will but driven by spiritual honesty, for the Catholic faith. The present Roman church is built in large measure on the results of his magnificent, lifelong campaign.

The power for this rebuilding came from within the older church itself. Ignatius Loyola and the Society of Jesus furnished that leadership. But the superb Loyola would have been burned, excommunicated, outlawed, and gone the way of the dove in the power of serpents, had not Luther brought down the Renaissance papacy.

It is foolish to say Luther was the first "modern" man, or to date the so-called modern world from the Diet of Worms in 1521. It is equally foolish to claim for Luther the consummation of Christian thought. He cannot furnish us with leadership in all things. Gone forever is the world in which he was born and worked. He was studying Paul's epistles while the Americas were being mapped. The Americas are mapped now—but Paul's letters still call for study.

Devils, witches, and the world of superstition were his native environment; he is not to be followed as a critic of folklore. But the devils in character were his chief antagonists, and these remain with us. In the Wartburg he may have thrown an inkwell at an imagined devil, but in the Wartburg he also translated the New Testament— an epoch-making, language-creating service.

He was never a fundamentalist, in the word's modern connotation. The Bible was to him the glorious and eternally true Word of God, but he exercised a sovereign freedom in interpreting it. Neither was he a humanist; the all-creating, all-sustaining, all-merciful grace of God excludes a humanistic basis for theology.

Luther was a man of his own day. Rough, strong, boisterous, he knew he and his Germans were unlettered and uncultured. But he knew also the sweet gentleness of friendship and affection, the strong attachment to hill and valley, the haunting comfort of music. He knew the hatreds, prejudices, sciences, philosophies, habits, and pleasures of Saxony in the year 1500.

But in terms of the external, Luther was free, transcending all things constricted by time and custom. He knew the Hebrew prophets, the church's first evangelists, the martyrs, bishops, and saints of Christian history. He wrestled with the moral law and came to understand the first great principle of all ethics: that humankind, not law, is the objective. He tuned his inner life to the rhythm of the Psalms and knew their midnight cry for aid. He centered his life and thoughts in the Lord of Christian hope. The humanity of Jesus was the foundation of his faith, the key to all his theology.

Were Martin Luther to speak to us again, we would hear the old, old plea of the believing heart to hold by faith to the truth of the historic life of Jesus, to move by faith from this to its high implications for the character of God, and to live by faith in the eternal, blessed communion of the timeless City of God.

To see him grow into the beauty of the church; to watch him win the personal faith of Christian experience; to be present while he feeds his sheep in lecture hall, confessional, and pulpit; to see him battle for the honor and purity of the faith; to know him standing in quiet, stubborn peace, as the martyrs of old, before the rulers, affirming the sufficiency of his faith; to walk with him through the long, difficult years after the glamor and shouting; to hear his cradle songs of Christian beauty; and then to see him die, his heart unshaken—is this not enough?

In a world of swift changes, Luther sought and held steadfast the ancient truth.